Third Heaven, Angels and... Other Stuff

"Pat Coking is a beautiful Christian whose heart is for everyone to know and experience the God of the Bible. This book will lead you to places in God you didn't know you could go. When you experience God in the ways described in this book, your daily life will feel the impact and, like Pat, you will be the kind of Christian that others can follow" (1 Cor. 11:1).

WESLEY AND STACEY CAMPBELL, REVIVAL NOW MINISTRIES

"I love this book! I find the teachings and guidelines a must for all who desire to experience the open heaven and the supernatural...."

TODD BENTLEY, FRESH FIRE MINISTRIES

"Pat skillfully teaches and motivates through personal stories as she ministers to YOU in this book—showing how you can both experience and understand the "third heaven"—the very thing many of you have been asking God to let you do!"

STEVE SHULTZ, THE ELIJAH LIST

"As a gifted revelatory teacher, Pat Coking approaches this delicate subject with a sensitivity and creativity that unleashes hunger for the supernatural. Her personal experiences coupled with her keen insights into the Word make this a compelling book that will ruin you for the ordinary."

JILL AUSTIN, MASTER POTTER MINISTRIES

"We highly recommend this book. As you read: you will laugh, you will ponder, you won't be able to put it down, but you will surely be spurred onwards and upwards."

PETER AND ANNE MARIE HELMS, THE RECABITES

"I am sure that this book will be of great help for any Christian who is honestly seeking to grow in the prophetic and apostolic ministry."

WALTER HEIDENREICH, FCJG

"This book is helping the Church to enter into a spiritual land that has been vacant during the last centuries. Let your faith be stimulated to trust for new levels of His presence."

MICHAEL SHIFFMANN, TARGET EUROPE

PATRICIA KING
(PAT COKING)

THIRD HEAVEN, ANGELS AND ... OTHER STUFF

Belleville, Ontario, Canada

Third Heaven, Angels and... Other Stuff

ISBN: 1-55306-403-8

First printing, August 2002
Second printing, June 2003

**For more information or
to order additional copies, please contact:**

Christian Services Association
2041 Harvey Avenue, Kelowna, B.C. Canada V1Y 6G7
Phone: (250) 765-3423 • *www.patcoking.com*

Essence Publishing is a Christian Book Publisher dedicated to furthering the work of Christ through the written word. For more information, contact:

20 Hanna Court, Belleville, Ontario, Canada K8P 5J2.
Phone: 1-800-238-6376. Fax: (613) 962-3055.
E-mail: publishing@essencegroup.com
Internet: www.essencegroup.com

Printed in Canada
by

Essence
PUBLISHING

Dedicated to my husband Ron who:

Is from heaven,
Is an angel,
and
Put up with a lot of stuff
as I wrote this book.

Table of Contents

Foreword
by Donna Bromley

I have personally read many books about the lives and experiences of the Christian spiritual mystics. Quite frankly, most of them depress me as much as they inspire me. Their heavenly experiences seem so tantalizing to a heart hungering for more of God. Yet, as I delve deeper, I discover that these mystics were often quite eccentric, spending years in self-mortification and celibacy in order to attain the experiences of heavenly ecstasy they describe. Fortunately for all of us, none of these characteristics describe Pat Coking!

This book is as refreshing as the title suggests. It is "down-to-earth" (at least until you put it into practice!), full of personal experience that inspires faith, witty (yes, Pat, you really are quite funny), and biblically sound (which is important if you are planning to venture into the realm of spiritual experience). Finally, a book that takes the mystique out of the mystical and makes it user-friendly.

Over the years that I have had the privilege of walking closely with Pat I have been deeply impacted by her walk with the Lord. Pat Coking is, before anything else, a radical lover of God. Her passion and loyalty to Him is unwavering. As a seasoned apostolic and prophetic woman, her faith has been forged through years of trials and testing on the front lines of Christian ministry as she "takes the Kingdom of God by force." Pat is also one of the finest teachers of the Word of God I've been privileged to learn from. She lives in the Word and the Word lives in her.

Today, heaven and earth seem to be drawing closer together. With every new wave of God's Spirit there is a need for an apologetic that will keep the Body of Christ safe while they venture forward into new territory. We are living in extraordinary times and God is restoring to His people the experiential dimensions of their faith. The divine intersections of spirit and truth are creating explosions of revelatory experience that demand solid biblical foundations.

Many false religions and ideologies have ventured into the realm of the metaphysical. Christians, desiring to stay clear of dangerous and erroneous practices, have often "thrown the baby out with the bathwater." Rather than being scared off by the fear of illicit spiritual experience, it is time for the Church to understand what rightfully belongs to her as children of the Living God.

Pat's motivation in writing this book is to encourage *all* of God's people to eagerly pursue spiritual experience the same way we enter into all other aspects of our Christian life... *by faith.* I believe Pat is also motivated by a deep sense of responsibility to keep the people of God *safely grounded* inside the boundaries of Scripture while they learn to live with Christ in heavenly places.

Perhaps our ability to access this supernatural realm of the Spirit will be the very thing that enables us to stand and overcome in the trying days ahead. Who knows—it might literally save your life. As you'll see in a coming chapter, it possibly did mine!

About Donna Bromley

Donna, along with her husband Ralph Bromley, President of Hope for The Nations, serves on the pastoral and core leadership team at New Life Church in Kelowna. Both Ralph and Donna have traveled extensively throughout the nations and have been used to establish numerous children's homes. They have a passion to rescue "children at risk."

Donna, with Pat Coking, is co-founder and overseer of the War Room, a house of prayer committed to praying for global revival and harvest. She also oversees the intercession department at New Life Church and is trusted for her prophetic accuracy in prayer. Donna is sought after as a conference and seminar speaker.

Introduction

All around us we see people increasingly intrigued by and hungry for spiritual things. An emphasis on materialism, career, and education in our society has, for the most part, left the masses feeling empty and longing for purpose in life. The youth of today are generally fearful of the future and long to give themselves to something meaningful. They want something they can live for—something they can die for. As a result, we are seeing the emergence of spiritual awakening.

Consequently, we have now entered an era of transition. Signs of this transition are everywhere. Many books and movies today have a spiritual theme. The New Age has infiltrated the schools, the medical profession and the business world. Children's programs, cartoons, and games are often supernatural in nature. Satanic, occult, and New Age groups are growing dramatically as they continue to introduce hungry new "converts" to the spirit world. Where is the Church in the midst of all this counterfeit uprising?

Over the years, I have witnessed a great deal of fear in the Body of Christ concerning supernatural activation and experience. It is imperative that we explore the Word of God, discover what is rightfully ours in Christ, and lead the way into this new era of spiritual reality. How will we ever learn to discern the counterfeit if we are not familiar with the "real thing"? How will the unsaved ever embrace the truth if they only know the false?

My passion in writing this book is to awaken a hunger in believers for all that Scripture offers us—intimacy with Jesus and authentic spiritual experience. I also desire to turn the hearts of believers to the foundation of the Word as a basis for all Kingdom encounters.

We will definitely need to live from a "third heaven perspective" in the last days. There will be turmoil and treachery in the earth, but we, the glorious Church, are seated in heavenly places in Christ (Eph. 2:6). We are to live our lives from a different "viewpoint" than those without Christ. We are to be a people who are focused on the heavenly and the divine. *"Therefore if you have been raised up with Christ, keep seeking the things above, where Christ is, seated at the right hand of God* (Col. 3:1).

Oh, that we would truly be such a people!

Third Heaven, Angels and... Other Stuff

Have you ever imagined yourself eating and drinking with God on sapphire streets, entering a glorious cloud of His Presence, gazing at the Lord high on His throne while His kingly train fills the temple, or personally encountering angels? Have you ever, in your wildest dreams, contemplated the possibilities of literally outrunning chariots, observing the armies of heaven in action, being suspended between heaven and earth by the locks of your hair (like Ezekiel), or being supernaturally transported from one geographical location to another by the Spirit of God?

Do these experiences sound "way out" and unattainable for the average believer? Should these types of divine events be "commonplace" for us? Dare we believe for a life filled with such supernatural occurrences as we find in the scriptural examples we have just mentioned? And if so, why should we?

How could traveling in the spirit, seeing an angel,

or hanging out in the "throne zone" enhance our worship of the King of Kings in any way? How could such experiences possibly make us stronger Christians, and deepen our intimacy with Jesus?

In this book, we will discover through Scripture that such encounters are not only attainable in a believer's experience, but that the Lord actually *desires* us to participate with Him in supernatural Kingdom life. If you are desperately hungry and thirsty to experience more of God and His realms of heavenly glory, then read on. If you find no such desire within, then perhaps you shouldn't. Or—hmmm—perhaps you should.

Heaven, Angels, Firebombs, and Laughter

"The wind of the Holy Spirit is about to blow upon this section. Get ready, here He comes," declared the revivalist, just moments before the tangible blast of a powerful holy wind struck our seating area. I was suddenly whacked with the glorious impact of this "wind power" and found myself crashing between two rows of metal chairs; but oh, how marvelous it all felt! Before I could "get a grip" on what had happened, the revivalist called for all those who felt the Spirit's power to make their way to the front. He believed the Spirit desired to touch us again.

I honestly did not know how I could possibly make it to the front because of the weakness I felt after the mysterious blast of power overcame me, but I was determined to respond. I staggered forward and attempted to stand with others who were eagerly awaiting a second touch. Before another word was spoken, I fell down again under the power of the Spirit. This time I began to laugh loudly and uncontrollably!

My exuberant laughter in the midst of a public and solemn meeting embarrassed me, especially because I couldn't think of anything funny that would trigger my response. The more I attempted to arrest the hilarity, the worse it became. My mind and my heart began a wrestling match. My mind argued with the validity of such behavior while my heart delighted in the experience. A sincere question rose from my spirit as I recall silently asking, "Lord, exactly *what* is so funny?" Then I burst into hilarity again. These uncontrollable outbursts merely increased my inner wrestlings.

"I heard heaven laughing"

After numerous minutes of flailing on the floor and laughing explosively, the Lord in His goodness allowed me to enjoy a divine experience that I shall never forget. In my spirit, I found myself in the midst of heaven. I literally and audibly heard heaven laughing. It sounded like an enormous multitude of voices exploding in such convulsive merriment that I thought someone had just told a good joke. Heaven's atmosphere appeared to be like that of a vibrant party. To be honest, this was disconcerting to me. I remember thinking, *Is this all you do up here—party and tell jokes, while we are suffering greatly down on planet earth?* Despite my mental objections, my spirit was still enjoying heaven's elation.

What was amazing to me, though, was that every time heaven laughed, I would also laugh and every

"There was a divine connection..."

time heaven ceased, so would I. There seemed to be a divine connection between the laughter in heaven and the laughter that was inspiring my spirit. I had no idea what was causing this intense release of joyful emotion, but it did feel very good! Heaven was completely filled with joy and without a trace of concern or anxiety. All was at peace! Everything felt wonderful!

"Angels and hot coals"

Suddenly, I was taken up into a vision. I saw angels ascending from various locations on earth with coals in their hands. In heaven there appeared a large altar with a blazing fire on it. The angels brought the coals from earth and placed them on the altar. Somehow I knew that these coals were the prayers of the saints. In the fire, the coals grew much larger and became flaming hot. Angels took the coals from the altar and flew back to the earth with them in their hands.

In my vision, I saw black patches all over the globe. These patches were the locations of Satan's strongholds on earth. The angels began to throw their "firebombs" into fortifications of darkness and suddenly demons were scattered, fleeing in terror, and screaming in fear. Then I would hear the elated explosions of heaven's laughter. This fiery display reoccurred a number of times with heaven's demonstrative rejoicing accompanying each victory... and, every time heaven laughed, so also did I. The Lord reminded me of Psalm 2:4: *"He who sits in the heavens laughs, The Lord scoffs at them."* My body convulsed with hysterical joy at the very thought of the enemy's defeats.

"Heaven had made an impact on me"

This actual experience of "visiting heaven," during a revival meeting in Florida in January 1994, worked many deep things within my heart. First, God began to break my pride and soulish resistance to His manifested power. My spiritual eyes were also opened and I was realizing that there were heavenly parallels that coincided with my natural behavior in the earth. Heaven was having a profound impact on my life.

As a Kingdom child, I had experienced His power, His glory, and His heart. These revelations were completely new to me, opening a doorway, a portal, into experiences in glory. In the days that followed, I was to enjoy, as well as wrestle, with many supernatural occurrences. There would be many more visions, revelations, angelic visitations, heavenly experiences, power encounters, and supernatural phenomenon that would invade my Christian experience. This was only the beginning. The Lord was preparing my heart to receive more of Him. My walk with the Lord was to become more tantalizing, more intimate, and more glorious than I ever could have imagined.

On my return to Canada a few weeks later, I received a call from my good friend, Mary-Audrey Raycroft, who described to me how the Holy Spirit had been powerfully released in a fresh outpouring of grace in Toronto. "Oh my!" The multitudes were now experiencing spiritual phenomenon that would soon literally shake the Church on a global level. It seemed that masses were experiencing Holy Spirit-inspired laughter and responding in dramatic ways to His supernatural touch.

Things would never be the same. An unsatisfied hunger and thirst for His tangible Presence now burned inside of God's people. Believers were traveling from all over the world in planes, cars, vans, buses, and trains, to partake of this wonderful and glorious outpouring of the Spirit of God.

"Why?"... Because most believers are absolutely desperate to experience the Lord and His supernatural Kingdom in tangible and meaningful ways. Is this your passion and desire? Then get ready to be filled. Get prepared for supernatural and divine impartation as you continue to read. The Holy Spirit is longing to visit *YOU* in *POWER... fasten your seatbelt!*

Hangin' Out... in Ephesians 1:3

For weeks I had felt led to pray for a well-known prophet. Although I had never met him, I was aware of his respected international prophetic calling and was very stirred to pray protection over his life and ministry. Every time I began to intercede for him, though, I would feel waves of the Lord's presence and a welcomed sense of being "drawn into the heavenlies."

The times in prayer were pleasant and made me wonder if I was about to experience a season of being intensely aware of the spirit realm. These feelings seemed to sweep over me every time I prayed for this prophet. I understood that he received very vivid visions and frequent "trips to the throne room." He was also known to be extremely precise and accurate in his ability to hear from the Lord.

Insatiable Hunger and Sanctified Jaws

A thought crossed my mind one morning during my personal devotional time that perhaps when I gave myself to prayer for this prophet, I was actually receiving an overflow of some of his anointing and gifting. Now, *that* idea was something to ponder. If it was actually true, then I should indeed intercede more. "Give and it shall be given unto you, pressed down, shaken together and running over...'Yippee'!" I personally have an insatiable, holy hunger for the things of God's Kingdom, so when I see something "spiritually delicious," I most certainly open my sanctified jaws and go for it.

This overflow of impartation is possibly what happened to Elisha when he received a double portion of Elijah's spirit. Elisha had given his time and gifts to Elijah in selfless service and consequently we see the prophetic mantle of Elijah actually falling on Elisha when the whirlwind took his mentor up into heaven (2 Kings 2:11–13).

I am convinced that when you give yourself into any Kingdom assignment, you are "sowing seed." That seed will then mature, bear fruit, and multiply, eventually producing a harvest of righteousness (see 2 Cor. 9:6–11). When you give yourself in prayer or finances to someone's ministry, that seed of faith will reproduce and multiply itself. So, let's say that you were called to sow prayer into a person's prophetic ministry. You would begin to ask the Lord on that person's behalf for the increase of revelation, wisdom, dreams, accuracy, visitations of the Lord, and intimate moments of worship during personal devotional times. What you are actually doing through this focused intercession is sowing seeds of prophetic strength, character, and gifting into someone's life. What you have sown in faith and love you will eventually reap in your own life and ministry. I am not saying that you will necessarily carry the same call and mandate of the person for whom you are praying, but the essence of what you are sowing through your prayers (i.e., prophetic strength, gifting, anointing, character), will be returned to you according to the scriptural principle of sowing and reaping.

The Scripture also says,

> *"He who receives a prophet in the name of a prophet shall receive a prophet's reward; and he who receives a righteous man in the name of a righteous man shall receive a righteous man's reward"* (Matt. 10:41).

According to *Strong's Concordance,* the word "receive" in this particular context means: "to receive a person, giving him access to one's self; to lay hold of; to take possession of; to take with hand; to take to one's self; to make one's own, to claim, procure for one's self; to associate with as companion and attendant."

It could be said, then, that when you come alongside of a prophet or a righteous servant and associate with that person (possibly in prayer and financial giving) as a companion and attendant—giving access to one's self—you will actually receive or draw into yourself that with which he or she is blessed in Christ.

Following one particular time in prayer for this prophet, I experienced a delicate, sweet sensitivity in my soul towards "heavenly things." I began to meditate on the goodness of the Lord's promises and His incredible gracious invitation for us to experience life with Him for all eternity. As I continued to ponder this divine kindness, it was as though my emotions felt a deep touch of glorious—well, I guess you could call them just "great feelings." I literally felt the deepest part of my being drawn into the realm of His goodness and kindness. I took note of the sensation, and after the experience waned, I carried on with my day, performing chores while feeling extremely "normal."

Hot Buttered Popcorn and Crime Scenes

That evening the phone rang as my husband and I, along with our friend, Linda, were munching on some hot, buttered popcorn, totally caught up in an intense scene in one of my favorite television programs. (I'm crazy about shows where the bad guys are taken out by the good guys and righteousness triumphs over injustice—yeah!) Ordinarily, a phone ringing at such a pivotal place in a crime mystery would annoy me. However, this call happened to be from the daughter of a very good friend and co-worker of mine, Donna Bromley. Her tone was serious as she requested emergency prayer for her mother who had just been admitted to hospital. Her situation seemed grave—the medical staff suspected a pulmonary embolism. Understanding the seriousness of such a life-threatening condition, I was immediately overcome with a prayer burden. In the living room, seated in front of a cops-and-robbers show, just didn't seem to be the right environment to "pray through" this earnest call of intercession. Linda joined me as we quickly put on our coats and charged out the door for a prayer walk, determined to wrestle this through to victory!

At the time, I was in Mesa, Arizona, and this "power walk" took us down the main street of the city with four lanes of noisy traffic whizzing by. I must say that we were storming heaven in an exceedingly loud fashion as we violently claimed the Lord's promise of victory for our dear friend Donna. One of the Scriptures that came to me at the time was from Ephesians 1:3:

> *Blessed be the God and Father of our Lord Jesus Christ, who has blessed us with every spiritual blessing in the heavenly places in Christ.*

Inside Ephesians 1:3

Despite the heavy prayer burden, the meditation and confession of this particular portion of Scripture brought deep peace to me. I also began to experience the same divine pleasure on my soul that I had felt earlier in the day while praying for the man of God. In the very next moment, however, I found myself "right inside" Ephesians 1:3. Now, doesn't *that* just about blow your mind? You are probably wondering at this point, *Now, what on earth is she talking about?* Hang in there with me for a while longer. Let me finish my little story—it actually gets wilder—and then I will attempt to give you some scriptural foundation for this experience.

While I was in my Ephesians 1:3 "spiritual experience," I continued walking down the street, hearing all the traffic sounds, and completely aware of my environment. In fact, I even remember saying to Linda, who was walking beside me: "Oh my goodness, I am in Ephesians 1:3!" Please understand that my body, mind, will, and emotions were all intact and very aware of everything around me. In my body, I was walking down the main street in Mesa, Arizona—however, in my spirit, I was somewhere else. I was actually *inside* the Word of God.

Jesus said in John 6:63, *"The words that I have spoken to you are spirit and are life."* The Word of God is not just print on a page. It is not mere language. It is substance! The written Word that we read in the Scriptures simply represents the actual substance of what is being communicated.

When I went into Ephesians 1:3, I was very aware of the reality of the "place" where I found myself. It was a spiritual place and in it were spiritual blessings of every kind. I saw the blessings of wisdom, grace, love, joy, reconciliation, prosperity, health, strength, and favor. Some individuals have asked me to describe what the blessings looked like. I find that question extremely difficult to answer, because these blessings were "spiritual." However, the Lord did give me an acute discernment or "knowing" which blessings were which.

The Holy Spirit's presence was very real to me at the time. I was aware that, as a covenant child, legal access to all of these blessings had been given to me. I also had the sense that I was to wait on the Holy Spirit to show me how to move through this experience and not grasp for control. While in this realm, a strong desire to respect, honor, and submit to His leading rose within me. The communication between the Holy Spirit and myself was spirit-to-spirit and no audible words were spoken. I knew what He was thinking and was aware that He knew my thoughts.

Depositing the Healing Blessing

The Spirit led me to take hold of the healing blessing. I did so. How? Again, that is very hard to explain in natural language. In my spirit I knew I was handling the substance of healing. The Spirit then directed me to deliver that healing substance to Donna, who was about 1500 miles away, in a hospital bed in a city in Canada! Immediately I found myself (in my spirit) hovering over Donna in the Vancouver hospital. Please take note that this experience was in the spirit realm. I did not speak to her or have any interaction with her, but I did deposit the healing blessing. This deposit was accomplished solely by faith and obedience, a release of faith in response to the leading of the Holy Spirit. As soon as this transfer of faith took place, I knew she was healed and I was immediately "back" in Mesa, Arizona.

No Time or Distance in the Spirit

In the spiritual dimension there is no time or distance. When you are in the spirit, you can be in one place one moment and in the next moment somewhere else. Ezekiel the prophet experienced this spiritual travel when, as recounted in Ezekiel 8, he was taken by the Lord into the innermost part of the temple to see the corruption. John the Beloved, while on the Isle of Patmos, experienced an immediate "trip into the glory realm" in Revelation chapters 1 through 5.

The principle of no distance in the spirit is true in the soul realm also. For instance, our family had the privilege of living in Hawaii for 7 months about 22 years ago. We are not in Hawaii at this particular time. Although my body is currently in Canada, my mind can be in Hawaii right now if I choose to think about it. Oh yes, I can see the powerful waves rolling in on the white sand. I can see a vivid picture of the palm trees and the luscious tropical vegetation. I can almost even smell the coconut-scented suntan oil. My thoughts are in Hawaii, but my body is not. Thoughts are part of the soul. The body is what restrains us to the principle and law of distance. Soul and spirit, however, are not bound in that way.

Time has no influence in the spiritual realm, either. Time is actually a substance within the eternal dimension. When you are in the spirit, you are able to see into the past, the present, and the future as the Holy Spirit directs. Daniel, for instance, saw into the future when he prophetically viewed the end-time visions in the book of Daniel. So also did John as he scribed the visions we see written in the book of Revelation. I believe Moses saw into the past when he wrote the book of Genesis. He was possibly shown those details by God when the Lord revealed the "back parts" of His glory in Exodus 33:23.

"Crunchies"

During the entire spiritual encounter and while depositing the healing blessing, I had continued walking and was still aware of my natural surroundings. However, I must admit, from time to time I stopped, engaged in a few "crunchies," spun a bit under the anointing, and then continued on. (Oh, by the way, a "crunchie" is the name some of us have given to a response of the body that comes from the manifestation of Holy Ghost power on your flesh... you "crunch"... the power makes your stomach muscles tighten. Sound weird? It is... but it sure feels good!) I even continued talking to Linda during this time. I said, "You'll never believe this: I actually went to Vancouver and gave Donna a healing blessing—she is healed!" I was confident that I was under the Holy Spirit's direction, leading and power the entire time. I did not feel at all separated from my body, although I knew that I was experiencing something in my spirit that my body was not.

Each part of our being (body, soul, and spirit) has a unique function. It is possible for each part to be engaged in different activities at the same time. For example, it is possible for your mind (part of the soul) to make a mental list of the things that you need to do that day, while at the same time, your body is experiencing something else—like a refreshing shower and shampoo. This example parallels spiritual experiences. It is not that the spirit has left the body; it is simply engaged in a spiritual activity while the body is engaged in a physical activity, and the soul is engaged in an intellectual or emotional activity.

I remained in the Ephesians 1:3 experience for about 40 minutes that evening. My sensitivity to the supernatural realm had waned a bit following my "return from Vancouver," but I still enjoyed fresh revelation of the Word of God and a strong sense of the Lord's presence as we completed our walk.

On our return home, following the prayer walk, I received a report that confirmed Donna was healthy and would be released from the hospital the very next morning. It is always nice to get the confirmations, but in this particular situation, I knew that I knew that **I knew** she was healed!

> *Blessed be the God and Father of our Lord Jesus Christ, who has blessed us with every spiritual blessing in the heavenly places in Christ* (Eph. 1:3).

New Creation Realities

I believe that the spiritual encounter that I just described will excite and motivate many to pursue deeper intimacy with the Lord and to search for truth. For others, my story could possibly create doubt, confusion, or even fear, especially if "new creation realities" are not fully understood. In 2 Corinthians 5:17 we read,

> *Therefore if anyone is in Christ, he is a new creature; the old things passed away; behold, new things have come.*

Spirit, Soul, and Body

We acknowledge according to Scripture that we are a three-part being consisting of a spirit, soul, and body (see 2 Thess. 5:23).

The creation account confirms this fact. In Genesis 2:7, the Scripture says,

Then the LORD God formed man of dust from the ground, and breathed into his nostrils the breath of life; and man became a living being.

We see in this passage that man was "formed" of the dust of the ground referring to man's physical make-up, his **body**.

Next, the Lord then breathed "the breath of life" into man. This breath of God became man's **spirit**; that is the principal life within him. This breath of life comes from the Lord of Creation and must not be confused with God's Holy Spirit who comes into His children at the point of new birth (see John 3:6). It was God's "breath" that created man's spirit or life. As soon as the breath of God entered the formed dust, a **soul** was produced.

The spirit of man relates to the spirit realm and is where our *God consciousness* dwells. It occupies the innermost part of our being and is sensitive and able to interact with the spirit world and with God.

The soul of man consists of our mind, will, and emotions and is *self conscious*. It is the seat of our personality. The soul is in touch with the relational realm. Intellect, thought, emotions, choice, decision, and imagination are all experiences of the soul.

The body of man, being formed of physical substance, relates to the physical realm and is more *world conscious*. It carries out the choices of the soul and is a container for the soul and spirit.

When a person is born again, it is the *spirit* that is born again. Jesus said in John 3:6, *"That which is born of the flesh is flesh, and that which is born of the Spirit is spirit."* At the point of being born again, Christ's Spirit enters a person's human spirit and they experience new birth. At that point, the person is a new creation and old things are passed away; all things have become new.

I clearly remember when I received Christ into my heart. I was completely convinced that I was different inside and yet *all* things had *not* become new. Even though I felt accepted, clean within, full of hope, and overjoyed at the thought of having my sins forgiven, I still had the same physical form and shape that I had before I prayed. My physical body hadn't changed one single bit (even though I would have welcomed that). My soul wasn't completely made new, either, for I soon discovered that some of my thoughts, attitudes, and reactions seemed to betray the Christ-like nature that I had been filled with.

You see, it is not our body and soul that are born again. It is our spirit. Our spirit man comes alive with the very nature and character of Jesus Christ at the time of our rebirth. We become filled with His righteousness, His glory, and we are given everything that pertains to life and to godliness (2 Pet. 1:2–4). We are absolutely perfect and complete within our born-again spirit nature.

Salvation is a gift and all Christ's glory and perfection is given to us by His grace. Your old spirit nature cannot be found after you are born again. It is like pouring yourself a cup of clear tea. After you have added cream, you can neither separate the tea from the cream nor the cream from the tea. You now have a brand new drink. The old is gone. When you receive the Spirit of Christ into your life, your spirit man becomes a brand new life. No longer can you separate yourself from Him or Him from you.

We are called to live by our born-again spiritual nature so that we will not fulfill the desire of the flesh. The spirit man, under the direction of the Holy Spirit, will eventually bring renewal to the soul if the soul follows the leading and unction of the born-again spirit. The soul is not to prevail over the spirit, but rather to submit to it. The will constantly makes choices of whether to follow the spirit or the lusts of the flesh. The decision is made in the soul. The body then carries out that choice. Let me further illustrate the principle of living by the leading of our born-again spirit.

I Was Spiritually Dull and Empty

In December of 2000, I was in the midst of a prayer retreat as is my custom every year. I was enjoying a month of personal devotion as well as a concentrated time of seeking the Lord for the word that He wanted me to carry in the next year as an itinerant prophetic minister. At this particular year's prayer retreat, I was feeling very dull and spiritually empty, even though I was diligently positioning myself for hours each day in prayer, study, and seeking the Lord's face.

Towards the end of the month I was feeling a little panic, for I had not yet received a clear word from the Lord for the new year. After I had pressed in for some answers, the Lord made it clear to me that He was going to lead me into a season in which I would not actually feel or experience His presence, His glory, or His love very much at all. He further revealed that I wouldn't even sense my own personal love or passion for Him. I would feel empty and lifeless and void of emotion.

"Why?" I asked.

"Because I am going to teach you how to live out of your spirit this year," He replied in that proverbial still, small, voice. "I am going to show you how to strengthen your spirit and in order to do so, I am removing your ability to lean on your soul or flesh."

Well, that sure didn't seem like it was going to be much fun. However, He was gracious to me, and gave me two keys to strengthening my spirit man. The first was to pray *violently,* using the gift of tongues every day. The second was to daily confess the covenant promises of the Word of God over my life. I soon realized that when you are void of emotion, there is no motivation at all to exert any kind of heartfelt energy, let alone violence. The exercise was good for me, though, because it forced me to live out of obedience to what the Lord had spoken to my spirit and not out of how I felt within my soul or body.

It was an interesting year. Many of my close friends were experiencing numerous manifestations of the glory of the Lord. My personal intercessor and longtime friend, Sharon Clark, phoned one day, absolutely thrilled to tell me about the visitation of the Lord's glory in her home prayer meeting earlier that day. She described in detail how each intercessor was deeply touched for hours by the glory that had manifested in the meeting.

No sooner had I completed that phone call than my co-leader in our prayer ministry in Kelowna, Donna Bromley, came by to visit—and believe me, she was a "shiner." She had a "glory glow" all over her and began to describe the wonderful downloads she was experiencing while in a deep, intimate place-of-heart connection with the Lord.

As for me, I was feeling dull, unaware of any strong sense of elation, and definitely not experiencing a "glory glow." Have you ever personally experienced times when you felt like you were the "wart on the Body of Christ"? You know what I mean—like everyone is getting touched, blasted, visited, glorified. As for you?... *Nothing... empty... dry*. It certainly does give you a tremendous opportunity to fight off rejection, isolation, and fear of abandonment. Anyway, as I was choosing to "rejoice with those who rejoice," a thought came to me: "I am just as much in the glory, in His presence, and in His power as they are, it's just that my soul and body aren't feeling it right now. It is all taking place in my spirit." This was not just a thought process I came up with in order to justify or validate my position as a cherished child of God. This was real, raw truth and I came undone at the very thought of it.

We are as complete as we are going to be in Christ. He is in us. He is the King of glory. He is the hope of glory. He **is** glory and **all** His promises to us as covenant children of God are *yes* and *amen*!

On the cross He has already secured for us every spiritual blessing in the heavenly places. He has given all things for us to enjoy. We don't have to hope and pray any more that we can get close to Him, feel Him, or receive one of His manifold blessings. He has already completed the work on the cross to give us access to everything in the Kingdom. This is so glorious. This is truth!

In the Glory Realm

The Lord is calling us all to live out of our spirits. In our spirits, we are already seated in heavenly places with Him. We are already in the glory realm. We are already in the throne zone (Eph. 2:5,6). In our spirits, we cannot get any closer to Him than we are right now. Our spirits are vitally and eternally one with the Lord and with His entire Kingdom. As we become acquainted with our spirit man, we will sense more of what is available to us in the glory realm, the spiritual realm.

It is the Word of God that rightly divides between the soul and spirit (see Heb. 4:12). Our born-again spirit will always adhere to the truth of the Word of God regardless of our thoughts, our feelings, or our circumstances. As we become more familiar with the operation of our spirit man, we will become more sensitive to God's Word, His will, and His ways. We will begin to experience and discern the supernatural as we become increasingly aware of our spiritual nature. Our emotions will be up and down at times. They can betray us. Our thoughts can deceive us. However, our born-again spirits are bound to, and are filled with, His presence and His truth.

The Lord had me journey through this "season of walking out of my spirit" for almost an entire year. Every once in a while, I would get a little reprieve, but for the most part, I was very aware of dryness and lived in a sense of feeling extremely empty. In the midst of this, though, the truth in my spirit rose up strong and embraced new creation realities. I didn't live out of my emotions—I had none. I didn't live out of my reasonings—they were confused. I experienced horrific levels of warfare to a point where every area of my life and ministry seemed to be challenged in deep and painful ways. Yet, my spirit remained strong. I always had the truth to lean on. I could live out of the safety and security of my spirit, where I held onto victory through it all.

By the end of the season, I had learned to love this walk of faith. It is not that I don't enjoy spiritual experience—I do. I am absolutely convinced that the Lord desires His children to enjoy experiential activity with Him daily. That is why I have written this book. More precious to me, though, is that His truth abides forever and will remain steadfast and immovable within our spirits, even if everything else in and around us is dull, dead, or shaky. We can be completely confident in our relationship with God as we seek Him for experience, whether we are touched in tangible ways or not. We have been truly blessed and filled with His greatness and glory. The Kingdom realm is home for us.

All that Christ is, we are in Him. All that Christ has, we have in Him. An invitation has been set before us as His dear and precious covenant children to explore the fullness of His presence. Let us then enter into the reality of the substance of the Word of God. Let us imbibe of all His blessings and experience His goodness; for we truly are a *"new creature"* in Christ Jesus; *"the old things passed away; behold, new things have come"* (2 Cor. 5:17).

Faith "The Connector to Heavenly Glory"

In the previous chapter, we discovered that all Christ is, and all He has, belongs to us in Him. Absolutely everything that pertains to life and to godliness has already been given to us through Christ's redemptive work on the cross. That includes the forgiveness of sin, mercy, provision, health and healing, strength, visitations of the Lord, His angels, His fire, His glory, spiritual vision, fellowship with the Holy Spirit, and everything that we need to live a fulfilled and victorious life in the Kingdom of God.

> "A little connector called faith"

The question for many is, "How do we secure the blessings in the heavenly places into our everyday life here on the earth?" The answer is simple: "By faith." Faith is the connector that secures all the covenant blessings, wrought through Christ's finished work on the cross, into our everyday lives.

It is extremely important, then, that we understand how to release our faith in order to experience the realms of heavenly glory. How do we access the throne of grace? By faith. How do we engage in communion with God? By faith. How do we enter the glory cloud? By faith. How do we see angels? By faith. How do we sense His presence? By faith. There is nothing too mystical about spiritual experience. It is all based on the infallibility of the Word of God and is accessed through a little connector called *faith.*

Faith is the foundational force that launches us into all Kingdom experience. Hebrews 11:6 says that,

> *without faith it is impossible to please Him, for he who comes to God must believe that He is and that He is a rewarder of those who seek Him.*

Hebrews 11:1 declares that, *"faith is the assurance of things hoped for, the conviction of things not seen."* In other words, faith is the connector or the "downloader," so to speak, of heavenly blessings.

Throughout this chapter, we will literally engage in a dissecting class and will attempt to dissect faith. I remember loving biology in school, especially when we had the opportunity to take little animals apart and examine all their intricate organs, discovering how every part functioned. Welcome, then, to "Faith 101." Get your lab aprons on, because we are going to have a good look at faith.

Over 20 years ago at a conference in Vancouver, Canada, I heard a popular Christian preacher share a sermon on faith. I have never forgotten that message and over the years I have meditated on it, acted on it, and developed it into a teaching that has now since been shared all over the world. The following is a brief overview of that teaching. The fuller development of this vital doctrine will be found in a subsequent book.

All right, are you ready to start dissecting? Here we go!

Faith Hears

Romans 10:17 tells us, *"So faith comes from hearing, and hearing by the word* [rhema] *of Christ."*

Faith comes through a posture of hearing and listening. In the New Testament Scriptures, two Greek words are rendered "word" in English. One is *logos* which refers to Scripture and to the revealed Word of Christ found within the written Word. When Jesus is referred to as "the Word" in the Scripture, He is called *the Logos.*

The other Greek word is *rhema,* which refers to the "quickened word" that comes to us by the Holy Spirit. When "word" is used in reference to Holy Spirit, it is usually the *rhema.* Ephesians 6:17 states that the *"sword of the Spirit"* is the *"word [rhema] of God."* The *rhema* is a quickened word for a specific situation and is brought to us through the inspiration of the Holy Spirit. It might involve the inspiration of an actual Scripture (*logos*) or it could be a word of knowledge, a prophetic word, a still small voice, but it will always be that which produces faith for the victory or provision of Christ in a particular situation.

"Our son was in trouble"

While in his early teens, one of our sons was getting into some trouble.

In discovering the details, we sat him down to talk him through it, and though he was very polite and agreeable throughout the discussion, we were unable to thwart the escapades. He continued on with the activities that concerned us. Some of these things were life-threatening and illegal. I was a seasoned prayer warrior at the time—in fact, I had taught seminars on prayer and led intercession meetings for years. During this season I applied all I knew in the area of prayer and yet everything seemed to get worse. In the midst of it, I assumed a position of absolute panic and terror most days. I would pray with intense emotion and seem to never hit a breakthrough.

Anxiety was filling my life, my thoughts, and my emotions, and I was getting very worn out in the battle. It is extremely difficult to see your children involved in dangerous things. You love them so much and want them safe and secure, hidden in the love and righteousness of the Lord. Anxiety, fear, and panic are all symptoms of unbelief and certainly resist the function of faith. Anxiety and fear were actually working against me.

One night I was wailing out with great intensity and unable to pray through to peace. Everything concerning my son's activities had become exponentially more difficult. In the midst of my travail, a Scripture was powerfully quickened to me out of Isaiah 59:21. I looked it up and read it with anticipation:

> *"As for Me, this is My covenant with them," says the LORD: "My Spirit which is upon you, and My words which I have put in your mouth shall not depart from your mouth, nor from the mouth of your offspring, nor*

from the mouth of your offspring's offspring," says the LORD, "from now and forever."

Oh my goodness, I thought I was going to explode! The promise was so alive, so real! Faith entered my heart at that very moment. It was unshakable. I had complete and total confidence that my son would be rescued and protected. All fear and panic fled in the presence of faith. I knew and believed, without a shadow of a doubt, that he would live secure in the blessings and mercy of God. I remember leaping up out of my chair at that very moment and speaking right into the face of the enemy: "You cannot have my son, for he is a covenant child. You will be sorry you ever tried!"

In the weeks that followed, our son's situation did not noticeably improve, but my reactions had certainly changed! Even though the promise hadn't manifested yet, I knew that it was a done deal. "Why?"—because faith hears. I had heard the voice of victory. I securely possessed the promise of God that insured the blessing. The victory did unfold in the months to follow and our son was fully restored. The battle, however, was won in prayer that night when faith entered via the "Sword of the Spirit." As the Scripture says, *"this is the victory that has overcome the world—our faith"* (1 John 5:4).

Our son's breakthrough came when I found one of God's covenant blessings and then called it down from heaven to earth. It was faith that drew the reality of that promise into my struggle in the earthly realm. Faith secured the heavenly substance of victory. In any of our life situations, faith can hear what the Spirit says to the Church... and to our hearts!

In order to "hear" the Word which produces faith, we need to posture ourselves in His presence. The story of Mary and Martha is a perfect example of a posture that anticipates and welcomes "hearing" from the Lord. We find that Mary took that position. She sat at Jesus' feet while Martha was "distracted" by her many preparations. It is important for us to take time out of the busyness of our day to "sit at His feet" and listen to what He wants to say to us.

Like the Old Testament prophet Habakkuk, we must also open our spiritual ears and position ourselves to hear from the Lord:

> *I will stand on my guard post And station myself on the rampart; And I will keep watch to see what He will speak to me* (Hab. 2:1).

Faith Sees

Faith always sees through God's eyes and from His perspective. In Genesis 13:14,15, we find God giving Abraham a faith vision. In this Scripture, God is speaking with Abraham after he had separated from Lot:

> *"Now lift up your eyes and look from the place where you are, northward and southward and eastward and westward; for all the land which you see, I will give it to you and to your descendants forever."*

In other words, He was saying, "If you **see** it, Abraham, you can **have** it."

Many times our vision is too small or it is distorted and so we fail and falter along the way. People often "see" themselves through a lying lens and thus believe they are failures, rejects, or worthless. Unfortunately, if that is how they truly **see** themselves, that is how they will be. As a man thinks in his heart, so is he! (See Prov. 23:7.)

Let us look at an example of how our mindsets influence our lives. The Scripture says that we are *"the righteousness of God in Him* [Christ]*"* (2 Cor. 5:21). Do you believe this? Do you see yourself in right standing with God, or do you see yourself always missing the mark and forever struggling with sin? If you view things from a negative vantage point, you will become what you believe or what you "see." If you see yourself as a sinner, you will sin. If you see yourself as righteous, you will live in righteousness. If the Word says you are righteous, you **are** righteous. Begin to believe what is true. Feed the vision of that truth into your heart.

Fact Versus Truth

There is a big difference between "fact" and "truth." It might be a fact that you committed a sinful act today. You don't need to deny that. You are free to acknowledge that, but it is only fact. Facts are temporal and truth is eternal. Truth always usurps fact. What is the truth in this particular scenario?

> *If we confess our sins, He is faithful and righteous to forgive us our sins and to cleanse us from all unrighteousness* (1 John 1:9).

Finished. No guilt, no shame. You might say, "But I don't feel cleansed or forgiven." In the faith realm, feelings are not valid if they are contrary to the truth. You are absolutely and completely righteous in Christ. This is the truth whether you feel it or not. Truth prevails over the fact. Your actions and behavior will eventually come into line with what you truly believe.

Now, let's apply this principle to the realm of spiritual experience. Do you believe that you are a person who can experience the glory presence of God? Do you **see** yourself as a spiritually sensitive child of God? Do you believe that through the eye of faith you can **see** the reality of the truth concerning the throne room, the angels, and the glory cloud of the Lord?

Your answers to these questions will determine your experience of the supernatural realm and the sensitivity of your spiritual vision. Revelation 3:18 advised the Laodicean church to buy eye salve that they might see.

What are we seeing? Faith will see according to God's perspective. We can train and sensitize our spiritual vision by meditating on the Scriptures, allowing our vision of life, heaven, and the spiritual realm to be renewed by His Word. His Word carries final authority. If you "see" it in His Word, then you can believe for that blessing to be manifested in your life.

Faith Speaks

We always speak what we believe. Jesus said, *"the mouth speaks out of that which fills the heart"* (Matt. 12:34). The spoken word is very powerful and creative when it carries the breath of the Lord in it. Jesus said that the words He spoke were spirit and life (John 6:63). *"By faith we understand that the worlds were pre-*

pared by the word of God" (Heb. 11:3). When we confess or proclaim the truth about the glory realm, it begins to build a framework in the spirit and will literally have effect upon our lives.

Daily Confessions

My husband and I attempt to make confessions of the Word of God daily. We speak out the word of blessing over our lives, children, ministry team, and church. We confess the promises because we believe the promises. Begin to confess the Word of God out loud on a regular basis and you will find yourself strengthened in truth and sensitive to the spirit realm. Blessings will begin to "come upon you and overtake you."

For example, confess by faith that every time you enter into the "tent of meeting" (your devotional time with the Lord) the glory cloud descends upon you like it did for Moses. Continue to speak out that truth and you will be amazed at the eventual outcome. The promise will manifest. You will then most likely begin to actually sense the glory of God in your body and emotions. At first you might not feel or sense anything. Simply lock in to the promise by faith and confess the truth of the Word. You can count on His promises; they are your inheritance in Christ.

Here's an application. Do you desire to "experience" the throne of God? Then it's time to hear a word from God. Ask the Spirit to quicken a word to you, then begin to see the promise of God through the eye of faith. Ephesians 2:6 clearly states that we *"sit together in heavenly places in Christ Jesus"* (KJV). Where is Jesus? On the throne! (See Eph. 1:20,21.) Then where are you if you are indeed "in Christ"? Dare you declare it? All spiritual experience must be based on the truth of the Word of God. If the Word says that you are in the "throne zone," then you are! Your spirit man is already there.

Hebrews 4:16 encourages us to boldly come to the throne of grace so that we can obtain mercy to help in time of need. Do you believe this promise regardless of whether you feel it or sense it? Then, confess it. Speak it out: "Thank You Jesus, that I am at the throne of grace. I have accessed the throne room and am receiving help and mercy in my time of need." Why would we confess that? Simply because the Word says this is true and we believe it. Faith speaks. The more we speak out the Word of God in faith, the more we will see its manifestations.

Faith Endures

Galatians 6:9 declares, *"Let us not lose heart in doing good, for in due time we will reap if we do not grow weary."*

When we desire to enter into experiencing the spiritual realm, we need to be committed to standing on the truth of covenant promises, even at times when we feel spiritually dull.

In the last chapter, I shared my testimony of how I was called to live the truth in my spirit by faith, even when everything in my circumstances, emotions, and body felt shut down. Although the truth regarding the tangible glory presence of God had not yet manifested in my life, it still remained very true to the Word. I locked in to the truth and endured until the promises manifested.

We often give up in our faith walk when it looks like the promise is never going to manifest. God wants us to endure and stand in faith even when things don't look like they are lining up with His promises. Abraham endured even though, in the natural, his wife was beyond childbearing years. Many heroes of faith found in Hebrews chapter 11 went to their graves believing and not receiving the manifestation of the promise, but they went home in faith, while the promise of the Messiah manifested in the "fullness of time." It was the faith of these "heroes" that made the connection for that ultimate "download." They believed, right up until their last breath this side of time. They carried the truth in their hearts by faith, never doubting throughout their lives. Their faith greatly pleased the Lord. Faith endures.

Faith Receives

Faith also receives the reality of the promise, even before it is manifested in the natural realm.

> *"Therefore I say to you, all things for which you pray and ask, believe that you have received them, and they will be granted you"* (Mark 11:24).

All the covenant promises regarding the glory realm are secured into our lives by faith. Faith is different from hope. We are not hoping to have experiences in the glory realm. We believe that we are in the glory realm because the Word says we are. There is a big difference. Hope never secures the promises. Faith does. The receiving dimension of faith is literally how we lay hold of the blessings.

I remember a number of years ago hearing a testimony from an acquaintance of ours. Her eleven-year-old daughter had been learning from her Sunday school teacher how to receive by faith. The child asked her mother one day if she could have a piano because she wanted to worship Jesus with it. Her mother explained that they couldn't afford a piano at the time. However, she encouraged her daughter to pray.

The daughter went into her room and prayed a simple prayer: "God, I know that You've got lots of pianos in heaven and so I was just wondering if You could give me one?" She remembered Mark 11:24, a Scripture verse she had learned in Sunday school. She firmly believed that when she prayed, she received.

Following her time of prayer the child ran out to share her exuberance with her mother. "Mommy, Mommy, God just gave me a piano."

"He did?" her mother inquired. "Where is it?"

"Oh, it is in my spirit," replied her little girl. "I have a piano from God by faith." The mother was touched by her daughter's adorable behavior and "imaginary piano." She thought no more about her daughter's confession and did not actually take the faith project that seriously.

A few days later, the family went to church. Following the service, the church pianist approached the daughter, saying, "Honey, this week was my birthday and my husband bought me a new piano for a present. I was going to sell my old one, but as I was praying about it, I felt the Lord move my heart to give it to someone as a gift. I believe He said I was to give it to you. Can you use a piano?" The little girl was excited and blessed but not at all surprised. She had already received her piano before it manifested. She had learned the powerful lesson that "faith receives."

This is a simple illustration, but it is an example of how to secure all of heaven's blessings for your life. When you pray, believe that you are receiving and you will have what you believe if it is according to the promises of God. Faith receives.

Soaking and Receiving

A dear friend of ours, Todd Bentley, is a young, fiery evangelist who discovered a powerful way to receive. He grew up in very difficult and tragic circumstances and, in his early teens, was involved in crimes and confined to a juvenile home for a season. Todd was transformed by the power of the Lord's saving mercy when at age 18 he found Christ. Immediately he received evangelistic passion. He was hungry for everything that the Lord had for him. He daily devoured the Word of God and became intimately acquainted with the Holy Spirit. Todd was full of fire!

After a few years of serving the Lord, Todd had to take time off work due to a job-related injury, so he determined to use the hours he had free to seek the Lord. He now refers to this period as his "soaking season." For hours every day he would put on a worship CD and sit before the Lord and "soak." He has testified that at times during the first number of hours he would not feel the Lord's presence, but he continued to wait on the Spirit, believing that he was receiving of the glory of God. He soaked in faith and received of the substance of heavenly glory. By faith, he was "drinking out of a glory well." Jesus said in John 7:37, *"If anyone is thirsty, let him come to Me and drink."*

Day after day, he would seek the Lord in this fashion. Before long he was experiencing third-heaven encounters, visions, and heart-to-heart dialogue with the Father. Today, Todd continues to spend time each day soaking in the presence of God and receiving the glory by faith.

As a result, Todd is passionately ministering salvation, healing, deliverance, and signs and wonders to the multitudes all over the world today. He simply ministers out of what he sees his heavenly Father do in heaven. How? By faith.

Faith truly is the connector to heavenly glory. Without faith you will not see God and you will not experience the Kingdom realm.

With faith all things are possible. Only believe. Faith **is** the connector to heavenly glory!

Lightning Bolts and Mongolian Dragons

During our first year of full-time itinerant ministry, my husband and I were seldom at home (we are actually at home even *less* now). After returning from one of our ministry trips, we decided to invite some of our prophetic friends over for an evening of fellowship and to get a pulse on what the Lord was saying to them and to our region.

As the time approached for our guests to arrive, I was preparing some coffee and goodies when the Holy Spirit spoke to me and said, "I don't want you to share with each other, pray, communicate visions, or even worship unless I direct you. Be still and wait for my unction." Well, *that* was a surprise. I had anticipated a rather exciting evening of sharing and fellowship, and now it sounded like God's agenda was possibly one of stillness and quiet meditation.

One of the most important keys to spiritual experience is to submit yourself completely to the leading and guidance of the Holy Spirit. He is our helper and teacher.

He leads and guides us into all truth and is our personal Mentor in spiritual experience as we get to know Him. He is not a mere influence or power, but a Person. He is the Spirit of God!

Comprehending all of this, I submitted to His direction that evening, even though I did not understand it. As our guests came we greeted them, and when all had arrived, I shared what the Holy Spirit had spoken. I instructed, "Let us not pray, sing a song, prophesy, share a vision, or even read a Scripture unless the Holy Spirit directs. We will simply wait on Him. If, however, He does nudge you to initiate something, then go for it."

Waiting on the Lord is quite a discipline because, most of the time as Christians, we are not comfortable with stillness and quietness. We tend to want to say something to break the silence. We all agreed wholeheartedly to follow His leading. Isaiah 40:31 states,

> *Yet those who wait for the LORD*
> *Will gain new strength;*
> *They will mount up with wings like eagles,*
> *They will run and not get tired,*
> *They will walk and not become weary.*

(Eagles are often a symbol of prophetic ministry and unction in the Scripture.)

As we were *waiting,* it wasn't long before someone felt led to pray, then someone else was inspired to sing a song. The Spirit's presence rested on us and, as we followed His leading, we began to enjoy a very sweet time of fellowship. We began to operate in prophetic giftings under the noticeable weight of His glory.

Lightnings!

As we continued to submit ourselves completely to His leading, suddenly a vivid flash of light came from the center of the ceiling in the room. It appeared to be a flash of lightning, but we were *inside* the house. We had all noticed it and were pretty "flipped out" (you know—the "holy flips"). *Oh my goodness. What is happening?* we wondered. "It's lightning!" I exclaimed loudly.

Someone in our group, who wasn't actually a prophetically-sensitive person, but was there to serve the group that evening, said, "Well, perhaps it is a short circuit in the electrical system. There is a light in the center of the room, perhaps it just flickered from an electrical short." *Ohhh... whatever,* we thought! Although we were all (but one) convinced that it was lightning and an actual visitation from God, we agreed to honor the "skeptic." In order to eliminate any room for doubt, we shut off the ceiling light, leaving only a couple of table lamps and a few candles to illumine the atmosphere.

As we continued to wait on the Lord, another bolt of lightning flashed in the same place where the first had appeared. *Yikes—we* ***were*** *being visited by a divine sign and wonder!* Despite our excitement, though, the "skeptic" continued to question the phenomenon. "Well, what if it's still an electrical short and the table lamps are reflecting the light flash?" Skeptics are great, aren't they? They put our faith to the test—and that's **good** for us! Right? Right!

So, to further test this experience, we turned off the lamps and left the candles as our only source of light.

We continued to wait on the Lord and before long another lightning flash lit up the room, and then another and another. There were about six in total that evening. Our excitement rose to fever pitch.

As we continued to wait on the Holy Spirit, He gave us insight into the lightnings of God. Lightning in the natural supposedly brings order to ions (electrically charged particles) in the earth's atmosphere. This act in nature clears and freshens the air. Lightning also changes the molecular structure of soil. Farmers apparently welcome lightning because it causes planted seed to grow faster. Lightning will also strike the "highest place" and will often destroy whatever it hits. *Hmm... could this characteristic of lightning be a prophetic picture of the destruction of pride?* The Lord revealed many more things to us regarding His lightnings and gave us prophetic applications. We were then led into a prayer time to release His lightnings into His Church.

Another Wave

After a while, the tangible presence of the Lord seemed to wane and I thought that perhaps we could break for coffee. (I do have a particular fondness for coffee—only blessed and sanctified coffee though, of course!) Just as I was about to make the suggestion, one of our friends said, "I feel the Lord saying that if we continue to wait on Him, He will give us another wave of visitation." All right! That beats coffee any day, even if it *is* sanctified!

We continued to wait on the Lord, committed to

respond only to His direction and not to our own desires. As we followed His nudging, the tangible weight of His presence began to visit us once again. Unexpectedly, I proceeded to speak out in the gift of tongues (see 1 Cor. 12,14). I wasn't praying in tongues, it felt more like preaching in tongues. I could actually feel the strong "preacher" rise up in my spirit.

The unknown tongues sounded like some type of Chinese dialect. One thing was for certain, though, I had never spoken in this language or in this fashion before. Then others in the room began to join me, most of them speaking in various types of oriental-sounding syllables.

OK—Here Comes the Dragon!

After preaching in tongues for a while, I was suddenly aware that, in my spirit, I was in a Chinese village in Mongolia. I can remember the hillside vividly to this day, as well as the little homes and the dusty main pathway through the hamlet. I remember seeing people going about their daily routine.

I also saw into the spirit realm over the village. A very large, ferocious, green-colored dragon was hovering over the settlement and seemed to take its position right over the main street or pathway. I discerned that this dragon was a ruling spirit in Mongolia and was enslaving this village under the power of deception and control.

The dragon could not see me. I was above it, preaching up a storm in these "new tongues" with tremendous fervency and confidence. I could literally feel the strength and might of the Lord as I spoke. When God calls us to spiritual warfare, He wants to give us a heavenly perspective. It is a good thing to be above and not beneath when facing dragons. Right?

Ephesians 1:20–23 teaches us that Jesus is positioned in the highest heaven, far above all principality and power, and has put all things in subjection under His feet. In Ephesians 2:6, Scripture further teaches that **we** are actually **seated with Him** in the heavenly places. In this experience, I was clearly above the dragon spirit while making powerful warring decrees in unknown tongues.

In the vision, I suddenly saw the dragon begin to lose strength. It was as though the words in tongues were actual arrows penetrating its life source. It fell to the ground and appeared to die. Finally, I witnessed a tremendous outpouring of the Spirit fall over the region and the entire village came to Christ. The peoples' eyes were opened to see the truth. Through this experience, the Lord revealed that a battle had been won in the heavenlies and that harvest would break out for a season in Mongolia. Many in that nation would come to Christ during a season of grace.

Since that time, I have become acquainted with ministries that preach the gospel in Mongolia. They have reported amazing divine encounters in this country where a great harvest of souls is taking place with demonstrations of God's power in specific regions of the nation.

When you are in a heavenly vision or trance, the Lord gives prophetic interpretation and understanding of what you are experiencing. Sometimes the interpretation comes during the vision and at other times there is a need to seek the Lord for more understanding and insight following the encounter.

After this prophetic warfare experience, I shared the vision with my friends and we prayed for more insight from the Holy Spirit. As in this situation, the Lord will often take us into spiritual experiences to engage us in high-level strategic intercession and warfare.

Considerations

In Ephesians 6, Scripture instructs us that our warfare is against spiritual entities and not flesh and blood. A believer should never presume to fight a spiritual battle outside of the direction of the Lord of Hosts, our commander and chief.

Believers have been given *"authority... over all the power of the enemy"* (Luke 10:19) and should never be afraid of a demonic spirit. Colossians 2:15 makes it clear that through Christ's victory, demon powers have all been "de-feated" and "dis-armed" (they have no feet and no arms—ha, ha). All authority in heaven and in earth has been given unto Christ and we are in Him! However, we should never enter spiritual battles outside of the Spirit's endorsement and leading. Many excellent teachings regarding intercessory warfare and its treacheries are readily available at this time. It is strongly advised to have good foundational teaching on spiritual warfare before engaging in it.

We **must** be cautious when operating in **any** realm of spiritual experience!

Consecration Is Important

One of the greatest protections for Christians is to walk in consecration. *Consecration* means to be set apart as holy for God's purposes. In the Old Testament, when something was consecrated or sanctified (sanctified means the same as consecrated), it was no longer to be used for common purposes. If we desire to be spiritually safe within the realm of experience, then it is absolutely imperative that we are consecrated people. We need to keep our mind, emotions, and body untainted by worldly or sinful values and mindsets. Be extremely watchful: if you desire heavenly experience, you will require heavenly levels of consecration.

I am often deeply troubled when I see Christians compromising their sanctification with worldly passions. If you love worldly and fleshly passions, then your experiences in the spirit can be tainted by those compromises. I am not suggesting in any way that we establish a "code of righteousness." That would be legalism and religion.

True holiness involves loving all that God loves and hating all that He hates. The Lord will reveal His heart on these things as we spend time in intimate friendship with Him. Obedience to His "holy" directions will then set us apart for heavenly glory and empowerment. Joshua 3:5 confirms the importance of consecration: *"Then Joshua said to the people, 'Consecrate yourselves, for tomorrow the LORD will do wonders among you.'"* If you desire to experience divine signs and wonders, then consecration is vital.

Plumblines of His Word and Character

God has given us other important plumblines for evaluating: our experience must stay within the perimeters of the Word of God and must line up with the character of God. If your experience violates either of these standards, then it is not valid and could even be dangerous!

A recent movie gave me the opportunity of using some of God's plumblines. Christian friends had recommended it to me. Apparently, the script for the movie was a modified version of a book that had been written by a Christian author many years ago. Numerous Christian friends and leaders had told me that this movie was full of prophetic symbolism. They suggested that it was most probably inspired by the Lord as a standard against pervasive occultism in our society. Thrilled with the public exposure this movie was receiving, they strongly encouraged me to view it.

As a result of the encouragements, my husband and I raced out to the nearest theater to see it. However, the movie deeply grieved me. It only took half an hour to recognize the blatant occultism and vivid display of ***"good"*** witchcraft and sorcery warring against ***"evil"*** witchcraft and sorcery. It was all about occult powers wrestling with each other.

The power of good overcoming the power of evil was the basic foundational message (although at the end of the movie, the power of "good" still looked very weak and under siege—you had to watch the sequels in order to see the final victory).

When applied to situations like this, the Word of God is very clear—it absolutely forbids the practice of witchcraft in any form. Scripture actually says that the practice of sorcery and witchcraft is an abomination to Him (see Deut. 18:9–14). In the Old Testament, The Lord said that all witches were to be killed and that the land was to be purged of their presence (see Ex. 22:18). It is obvious that God does not want His Name or His Kingdom in any way represented by metaphorical figures involved in the dark arts. He would never endorse or affirm something that His Word forbids.

Prior to giving my heart to the Lord, I was searching for "answers to life." I went on a spiritual journey to find fulfillment. This journey led me to New Age and occult practices, one of which was "white" witchcraft. While practicing this "craft," I did not believe that I was doing anything wrong. After all, isn't fighting evil with good a noble thing? I wasn't cursing anyone. I was releasing "good spells" and "good potions." I was using "good prophetic senses" to reveal people's futures. My heart was to help and support people.

Following my conversion, the Lord made it very clear that these practices not only needed to cease in my life, but they needed to be renounced. Any manipulation of the spirit realm outside of the influence of the Spirit of God is witchcraft and is a forbidden practice. I needed to be delivered—and I was!

Don't Be Deceived

In the last days, there will be many deceiving spirits sent out to deceive even the elect if possible. The demonic realm is going to increase its lying signs and wonders, false prophetic, false apostolic, and encouragement of forbidden realms of spiritual experience. Many will be led into deception. In the midst of all of this we need to watch over our hearts with all diligence.

The Word of God is our plumbline. We must never compromise the standard of His Word while pursuing spiritual experience.

You might say, "Yes, but a powerful, well known prophet or leader said this and that." If prophets' or leaders' words or counsel violate the Word or the character of God, their revelation is to be discarded. Remember that "to err is human." First, learn to discern using the plumbline of the Word and character of God. This plumbline can be applied to all revelatory and spiritual experience.

Reflecting on the "lightning encounters" and the "wrestle with the dragon" that night in our home, I believe that our experiences were consistent with God's plumblines.

One More Wave of Glory

Toward the end of our evening's experience with lightning bolts and dragon-slaying, the Holy Spirit led us into one more wave of His glory. The glory came in the form of absolute rest of spirit. The weight of His presence rested on us like a heavy blanket. One could have fallen into a deep sleep (this is actually another spiritual experience—see Gen. 2:21). There was an inward sense of satisfaction and we all knew that our "visitation" with Him had concluded for that evening... although, He continued to inhabit each one of us. Even when we are not having a spiritual experience, He never leaves us and never withdraws His love. Christ is forever with us even when we are not aware of His manifested presence. How wonderful He is!

Our time together that night was absolutely remarkable from beginning to end. It was one of those memorable occasions that will never be forgotten. Lightning bolts, Mongolian dragons, and—oh yes—"blessed" coffee and fellowship. What an evening!

The Glory

"*I pray You, show me Your glory!"*—this was the cry of Moses in Exodus 33:18. What was this glory that the prophet was so desperate to behold? The Lord's response to him was this: *"I Myself will make all My goodness pass before you"* (v. 19).

The Lord's glory is His goodness. In this particular passage the word "goodness" is in a superlative tense and means that it is the most maximized goodness a person can receive. The Hebrew word for "glory" found in verse 18 is *kabowd* and refers to the Lord's abundance, riches, splendor, honor, copiousness, and weight.

When the glory visits, His goodness, abundance, riches, radiance, brilliance, brightness, preciousness, weight of presence, and the manifestation of His splendor and honor minister to you. Wow! All this is promised to every believer! As Moses beheld the glory of God while hidden in the cleft of the rock, so also shall we. The Lord desires each of us to know the tangible experience of the fullness of His abundance and goodness that is found in the face of Jesus Christ. This is His glory.

In John 17:22,24, Jesus says,

> *"The glory which You have given Me I have given to them, that they may be one, just as We are one;*
>
> *"Father, I desire that they also, whom You have given Me, be with Me where I am, so that they may see My glory."*

Jesus is actually saying that He was freely giving to us all the splendor, the abundance, the weight of the Father's goodness, the riches, and the honor that the Father had given Him. Jesus was praying to the Father, before His departure, that we would be granted the privilege to dwell with Him in the heavenly places, in the throne room, beholding and drinking of all of His goodness. Glory to God! We often read that Scripture and think that it will be fulfilled after we die and leave this earth, but this promise is for us as believers right now!

The glory that the Father gave the Son is ours and we can access it by faith. By faith we can behold Christ's glory in the heavenly places. This glory has been **given** to us. It is a gift and cannot be earned.

Created to Partake of His Glory

When God created the earth, everything was full of His glory. The earth was a very manifestation of the Lord's abundance and splendor. His Word and His breath called everything into being. All that was created came from the depth of His glorious creativity. Everything was alive and shimmering with His presence. The trees, the flowers, the birds of the air, the fish of the sea, and even the very atmosphere was charged and electrified with the Lord's brilliance and presence.

In the midst of all this splendor and beauty, God created man. He formed man out of the dust of the earth. The dust probably wasn't like the dirt that we are acquainted with today. No, it was more than likely glory particles brought into being by the breath of the Almighty. This was before the fall when God's glorious presence covered the earth. Man was formed out of glory substance—let's call it "glory dust"—substance that was full of the glistening presence of God. Into that form, God breathed the breath of His life and man became a living soul—a soul full of His radiance!

Man was a walking manifestation of the glory of God. He didn't need clothing made of fig leaves and animal skins. Why? Because he was clothed in scintillating and magnificent glory! Adam was arrayed in the Father's splendor, His honor, His riches, and His abundance. After the Lord created man, He placed him in the midst of His garden and gave every living thing in the earth into his care. He gave him all—His presence and His glory!

As we know, man fell from the glory of God because of sin (Rom. 3:23). God had instituted a plan to restore mankind to a place where he would once again imbibe of and enjoy His presence and magnificence. His plan culminated in Christ's work of substitution on the cross—however, even in the Old Testament the Lord reached out to manifest His glory to His people.

The Tabernacle of Moses

In Exodus 25, we find the Lord giving Moses the pattern for the tabernacle. He was to build it according to the plan. The tabernacle of Moses is a picture of Christ and his finished work on the cross. This was the place where God would commune with His people. In the New Testament, through the fulfillment of Christ's redemptive work, we see that God's place of dwelling with His people is in Christ, the true and heavenly Tabernacle.

The completion of the tabernacle of Moses is found in Exodus 40:34,35:

> *Then the cloud covered the tent of meeting, and the glory of the LORD filled the tabernacle.*
>
> *Moses was not able to enter the tent of meeting because the cloud had settled on it, and the glory of the LORD filled the tabernacle.*

Yes, the Lord's glory filled the place prepared for Him and led Israel as they went through the wilderness. The Scriptures go on to say, in verses 36–38, that the cloud of the Lord's glory led them by day and the fire of His glory led them by night. Their journey was under the direction of the glory and so will ours be if we will abide in and submit to Christ, who is the eternal Tabernacle.

The Glory in Solomon's Tabernacle

We have established that the Lord's glory is synonymous with His goodness. We find confirmation of this in 2 Chronicles 5 at the dedication of Solomon's temple. Solomon had completed the building of the extremely elaborate house of worship and had set the sanctified priests, musicians, and singers in position for this holy event. In verse 13, the Scripture describes how the worshippers together made a unified, powerful declaration of praise: *"He indeed is good for His lovingkindness is everlasting."* In verse 14, we read that the house was so filled with the glory cloud of the Lord that the priests could not stand to minister.

You will notice that it was the declaration of the goodness and lovingkindness of the Lord that ushered in the manifestation of the glory. This happened because His goodness *is* His glory. The priests did not declare, "The Lord is angry and His wrath is everlasting." They declared His **goodness** and **lovingkindness**.

In Moses' tabernacle in the wilderness, there was a room called the holy of holies. This part of the tent housed the glory furnishings of the temple: the ark of the covenant, the mercy seat, and the cherubim of glory. It was in this place that the Lord's *shekinah* glory (the revealed glory of God) was tangible. The ark of the covenant represented the covenant that God would make with man through Christ's finished work on the cross as He fulfilled all the law and the prophets. The ark to this day represents the Lord's unconditional love and symbolizes His relationship with us based on His unfailing love, proven through Christ's death on Calvary's tree.

The next piece of furniture the Lord instructed Moses to build in Exodus 25 was the mercy seat—it was to sit upon the ark. Again, God is making it clear to His people that His relationship with man would be based on His mercy demonstrated through Christ and not on His judgment. Above the mercy seat stood the golden cherubim with their wings stretched over all. Ezekiel describes the cherubim as angels who are called to be stewards of the glory (see the Book of Ezekiel, chapters 1–10). This inner sanctuary of the tabernacle was the place where God revealed His glory. The message is clear. The glory rests upon and is found in His unconditional love and unfailing mercy.

When the priests in Solomon's temple began to declare the goodness and mercy of God, His glory came and filled the house. This is also true for His new covenant temples. His glory will come and fill our "house" too if we declare His goodness.

I have personally found that, as I proclaim the goodness of God in my personal prayer and worship times, the glory often manifests. Sometimes the glory feels like a "weight of love," or a sense of goodness and peace, and other times shows itself through power or visions. The glory can manifest in many other ways. We will discuss this further in other parts of this book.

Words Can Have Profound Impact

Words are often very significant and powerful in releasing the glory. Words can have profound impact on our lives either for our benefit or for our disadvantage. I am sure that, from time to time, you have found yourself visiting with someone, entering the fellowship time feeling quite chipper but leaving oppressed because of the person's negative and complaining attitude. In such a case, the very atmosphere around you can be weighed down with heaviness. You might leave the time of fellowship feeling discouraged, wondering what happened to your joy. The negative words created an oppressed environment.

In the same way, if you are in fellowship and the words shared are uplifting and edifying, it seems to influence the atmosphere in a positive way and it has a favorable effect on your life.

Words, as we discovered in a previous chapter, are not just mere language—they actually represent substance. When you make confession of the goodness, love, and mercy of God, you will find that the glory will manifest. Sometimes, I will quietly worship and say, "I praise You, Jesus, for Your goodness. You are so good, so kind, so loving, so generous. You are full of light, brilliance, radiance, splendor, abundance, riches, and You are here right now to show Your goodness to me." I might go on for a long time simply meditating on and confessing His goodness. As I continue in this fashion, the glory often manifests.

Jesus is the fullness of the Father's glory. If you are in Christ, you are in the glory. You can enter into, and enjoy, the glory at any time you want. You were created by God to enjoy it. Let His glory fill you. Let His glory clothe you.

The Priests Could Not Stand

You will notice that as the glory filled the house in 2 Chronicles 5:13–14, the priests could not stand to minister. The weight of the Lord's goodness brought them down to the ground.

We see a similar incident in Peter's life on the Mount of Transfiguration in Matthew 17:1–8. Peter, James, and John had been invited by Jesus to accompany Him to the mountain where a divine encounter occurred. Jesus was transfigured (He began to glow with the glory) while Moses and Elijah conversed with Him. This was quite the experience. In the midst of the glory, Peter's visionary gifting, colored by his "soulishness," concocted a "great plan" of action. "It is good that we are here," he confidently asserted, before unfolding his vision of a tent-building ministry designed to contain the glory being revealed.

The Lord had His way of dealing with Peter on this. How? He simply increased the glory! He turned up the heat of His goodness and Peter fell with his face to the ground. Then the Lord spoke out of the glory cloud and set Peter straight. The fear of the Lord visited Peter and he subsequently experienced the touch of Jesus in a tangible way. When he looked up, he saw "only" Jesus. Nothing else around him mattered any more—suddenly he was very focused!

That is what the glory will do for you, too. Like Peter and the temple priests, when you encounter the glory, your flesh will become weak. The glory was so strong that the flesh lost its power to stand (or to "rule," in Peter's case). I like that way of having my flesh disciplined. More glory, Lord!

The Lord Speaks from the Glory

You will also note that it was in the glory that Peter heard the clear voice of the Lord. When you bask in the glory, you will hear the Lord speak to you, too. That is what happened with Moses every time he went into the tent of meeting. The pillar of cloud descended and the Lord spoke with him "face to face," as a man speaks to his friend (see Ex. 33).

The Lord Himself is the focus of the glory. The Lord Himself *is* the glory. Moses observed this. The priests at the dedication of the temple experienced this. Peter's encounter in the cloud left him gazing upon only One. Nothing else was important or significant. In the midst of the glory, he saw one Man and He heard one Voice. You will, too.

Daily Disciplines for Experiencing Heavenly Glory

Our experience in the glory is led by the Holy Spirit and is born out of relationship with Him. Daily spiritual discipline and exercise is advantageous in that it helps us to position ourselves before Him and to focus our attention on growing in spiritual awareness. Spiritual discipline and exercise will aid in bringing the mind, will, and emotions, as well as the body, into increased sensitivity to the glory realm.

Bodily Exercise Profits a Little

In our Western culture we tend to be very focused on bodily exercise. You can usually find health clubs, gyms, aerobic classes, and weight training instruction along with a variety of health food stores and diet centers in most communities. Many churches offer classes and programs to enhance the health and strength of individuals. Bodily exercise is beneficial and I highly recommend looking after the vessel that contains the glory, but the Scripture says that it only profits a little (1 Tim. 4:8).

Our Western culture also emphasizes academic exercise. We ensure that our children get a good education in order for their minds to be strong and well-exercised. We often shun, however, the suggestion to strengthen our spirit. It might be safe to say that the majority of the Western Church is more influenced by logic and reasoning than by spiritual inclination. We are often afraid and uncomfortable when encouraged to embrace spiritual encounters in the glory realm. Many fear that we might be falling into some New Age technique or occult practice.

Satan Is a "Copy Cat"

May we never lose sight of the fact that Satan is a counterfeit and a "copy cat." He has never created anything original. He copies, perverts, or defies the reality of valid practices in the Kingdom of God. There is a great need for the Body of Christ to raise up a standard against the counterfeit by manifesting the "real thing."

Our First International Outreach

I remember back to 1981 when my husband and I went on our very first outreach to another continent. We traveled to West Africa with Mary Goddard, founder of Christian Services Association and my mentor in the gifts of the Spirit. Mary, a dedicated and passionate woman of God, moved very powerfully in miracles, signs and wonders, and the prophetic. We were looking forward to learning a great deal as we served her in prayer and altar call ministry.

Mary always had a way of drawing out the full potential of those she was called to encourage in the things of the Spirit. Many are standing in significant places of ministry today due to her influence in their lives.

On this particular outreach, she literally "threw" me into the deep waters of preaching in churches and conferences and sharing the Word on a national television program—yikes! She challenged us to step out in faith and work miracles and move in words of knowledge and the prophetic. In retrospect, I can clearly see how the Lord used that outreach to prepare me for an international itinerant prophetic ministry.

Powers from the "Dark Side"

We did indeed see the hand of God do amazing things, but what impacted me most was seeing the absolute devotion and discipline of those who served in the dark satanic arts. These individuals were willing to do just about anything in order to enhance their spiritual empowerment.

We heard stories that we found unbelievable at first until we witnessed their confirmations over and over again. These ones who were caught in the deception of satanic cults were willing to eat anything, regardless of how vile it might be; perform any act, even though it could possibly cost them their lives (or the lives of others), and sacrifice however much it would take to accomplish the demands that their "demon powers" required of them.

They would fast for long periods, participate in horrifically evil ceremonies and rituals, and even dismember and offer parts of their bodies in order to increase spiritual power. These are only a few things. Space as well as wisdom would fail me in this book should I describe all that we heard and witnessed concerning the atrocities associated with these cult members.

What impacted me forever, though, was that these deceived people were willing to discipline themselves and sacrifice to any extent in order to advance the purposes of evil. Their goal was to gain more wicked spiritual power and authority in their lives. It is unfortunate to note that these ones in the dark arts were truly performing terrifying and horrific acts of supernatural evil power—lying signs and wonders!

Christian Zeal Makes a Difference

I did praise God for the zeal of the African Church, which was taking a stand of faith, authority, and perseverance in the spirit. We would hear them exuberantly praying and praising in the night. All through the day we would see evidence of true Kingdom passion in these precious believers. Their spiritual discipline and sensitivity made a big difference. Godly miracles and power evangelism were the order of the day for them.

In the midst of this faith-filled and spiritually perceptive environment, I couldn't help but see so clearly the general failure of the Western Church in its apathy and slackness concerning spiritual disciplines. We have within us real and true power to give hope and aid to the nations, and yet we appear to be so weak in commitment and spiritual focus.

Can you imagine the transformation in the Body of Christ should we discipline ourselves to grow in spiritual sensitivity? We the Church, are called to be a glorious, faith-filled, devil-stomping, power-releasing, miracle-working people. Yeah! Let's go for it, people of God!

Spiritual Disciplines

Although spiritual disciplines will fortify our will, develop our character, and hone our spiritual discernment, they will never produce the power or the glory. Experience in the glory is never "earned"; it is simply a gift granted by His grace and received by faith. We can, however, always anticipate the eventual manifestation of the power and glory of the Lord by posturing ourselves to receive.

We are living in a very treacherous hour. The powers of darkness are attempting to advance their outreach and increase the manifestation of their influence. With their deceptions, these powers are making their way into schools, the medical profession, the marketplace, the movie industry, and even the Church. They are committed to their cause. Are we as committed to Christ and His Kingdom? Are we as committed to strengthening our spirits for the purposes of His manifested glory in the earth as demonic cult members are to fulfilling the devil's evil purposes?

Developing Spiritual Sensitivity

The following are simple principles that you might find helpful in beginning to develop your spiritual sensitivity and in facilitating entrance into heavenly experience and empowerment. (More in-depth teaching and instruction can be found on our *Glory School* tape series. Order information is contained in the back of the book.)

1. Acknowledge New Creation Realities

It is vital to acknowledge that you have been born again and that the very nature and power of Christ resides within you. As a new creation in Christ, you have a spirit that is filled with every spiritual blessing in the heavenly places and you *are* sensitive to Christ's Kingdom and the heavenly realm. It is very important for you to embrace this truth.

2. Submit to the Spirit

Lay down your own "soul desire" to lead and rule your time with God. Submit to the leading of your spirit that is under the direction and empowerment of the Holy Spirit. Invite your spirit man to rise up and take its place.

3. Repent and Receive Forgiveness for Sin

Invite the Holy Spirit to convict you of any unconfessed sin. Sin can block your ability to receive, hindering your relationship with the Lord and others. Should any conviction come to your heart, repent and receive forgiveness. Now you are clean—do not continue to dwell on your sin or hold on to any guilt or shame. Meditate on the gift of righteousness that has been freely granted you.

4. Consecrate Yourself to God

Submit your entire being to the complete influence of the Holy Spirit. Your spirit is already very aware of the Kingdom realm, but your soul and body are not as sensitive. Sanctify your image center (imagination), thoughts, emotions, and body so that you will be ready to receive the impressions that the Lord desires to give you (more detail on this in another chapter).

5. Love and Revere the Holy Spirit

The Holy Spirit is your Guide, Teacher, Helper, and Mentor in spiritual experience. He will reveal Christ and His Kingdom power and glory to you in deeper ways than you can ever imagine. Become His intimate friend and submit to His leading and instruction.

6. Drink of Heavenly Glory

Jesus said, *"If anyone is thirsty, let him come to Me and drink"* (John 7:37). By faith, begin to drink and soak in heavenly glory. Drink of His truth and allow your soul to receive of all that is in the deep well of your spirit. When you "drink," you are drawing the blessings of God into your being. This is done in simple faith. Sometimes I will sit in His presence and say, "Oh Lord, I drink deep of Your love; Your love is so refreshing; I draw deep into the well of Your love; I receive its strengthening power."

While I am "drinking" I simply focus and receive (by faith) the spiritual "substance" that has been promised to me as a covenant child. After spiritually drinking of the substance of His love for a while, I might then take a "slurp" of His glory, or His faith, or one of the many other Kingdom blessings promised me. You can drink for hours if you like. It is easy and very powerful! The proud intellectual mind might resist this spiritual exercise, but the childlike heart loves it!

7. Pray in Tongues

The practice of praying in the Spirit will help build you up in your inner man and your most holy faith. Praying in tongues cultivates sensitivity to the spirit realm (Jude 20; 1 Cor. 14:2–4).

8. Study the Word of God

The Word is a lamp for your feet and a light to your path. You will not stumble when you obey His Word and remain within the perimeters of its wisdom and counsel. Meditate on portions of the Word and submit your "image center" to the visions within the Scriptures. It is especially helpful to meditate on the visions of the throne room as found in Revelations 4,5; Ezekiel 1; and Isaiah 6. Attempt to picture the images in the Scripture within your imagination and your thoughts. This practice will help your soul become more sensitive to the spirit realm. When you remain submitted to the Word of God itself in these practices, it provides safe perimeters for the imagination and mind to grow in spiritual sensitivity.

9. Devote Yourself to Prayer

Share your heart with the Lord—let Him know your desire to see the glory. Make "big" requests for spiritual experience. God hears your prayers and will answer as you pray according to His will. Be patient and relax, even if the answers to your prayers don't seem to appear right away. This practice of prayer will build relationship between you and the Lord. Pray also for the needs of others and believe for the advancement of God's Kingdom in the earth. At times, you might feel led to fast. This discipline will usually enhance your spiritual sensitivity and improve your prayer times.

10. Worship Jesus

Acknowledge His worth and His value. When you worship the Lord, you are offering Him *your* presence and He loves it! Just as you delight in His presence, so He also delights in yours. The proclamation of His glory and worth will often bring the manifestation of the sweetness of heaven into your midst. Worship of Jesus will maintain right focus in your heart.

11. Wait on Him

Rest, listen, watch. Jesus will reveal His heart and His glory to you. Believe that He is speaking to you regardless of what you feel or sense in the natural. Be restful and do not strive. Wait in silent expectation for Him to bring fresh revelation, vision, and insight to you. Savor His presence and delight in what He reveals to you. Try recording in a journal the special insights and nuggets that He gives and then meditate on those treasures throughout the day.

12. Respond

Jesus only did the things that He saw His Father doing (John 5:19). Obey His leadings and commit yourself to being aware of His presence throughout the day.

Now, are you ready for a little exercise session, a little activation? Are you prepared for a few moments of "spiritual aerobics" and muscle building? Alright! Gird up, and go for it!

Glimpses into the Third Heaven

"Hey Pat, I've been having awesome times with God in the third heaven lately!" a young minister exclaimed with great enthusiasm.

"What on earth is third heaven?" I responded.

This curious term, "third heaven"—along with testimonies of related experiences—was coming up more and more. At the time I seemed to be growing in spiritual sensitivity and had also already experienced the Ephesians 1:3 expedition and the visitation to heaven (see chapters one and two). This young man, however, implied that this "third heaven stuff" could easily be an everyday occurrence for believers. This suggestion, of course, piqued my curiosity and stirred my spiritual hunger. I also felt a certain "fear of the unknown" as well as some godly caution. I had many questions and, at that point, very few clear answers.

When in Doubt, Check it Out!

In the Book of Acts where we witness the Apostles preaching the gospel and manifesting its great power, we find the "new" revelation of the gospel they carried was offensive to many and triggered a great persecution. Like those offended in Acts, we often reject, or even take offense, at what we do not understand. Scripture, however, gives us an example of a people, the Bereans, who kept their hearts open to the Lord, searching the Scriptures daily to *"to see whether these things were so"* (see Acts 17:11). As a result, they were called *"more noble than those in Thessalonica"* (KJV). Notice the Scripture says that they examined *"the Scriptures daily to see whether these things were so"—not* to see if these things were *not* so. There is a big difference!

My personal questions and concerns about "third heaven" experiences took me on a journey through the Scriptures. As Christian leaders, we must be extremely careful and take sober responsibility to assure that we are teaching and modeling truth. Usually, believers will, with trusting hearts, follow leaders. In Church history we've seen calamities over and over again as leaders became careless in their Christian walk and doctrinal beliefs. As a result, many were shipwrecked. As we appraise experiences against the backdrop of the whole counsel of God, we will remain under His protective covering. We are responsible should we cause a "little one to stumble" (see Mark 9:42). Let us, then, walk carefully.

What follows is a mini-Word study which, I

believe, confirms and validates "third heaven" experience. (I would highly suggest that you engage in further personal study. Due to space consideration, I can only give a brief outline here. The *Glory School* tapes and study manual will also give you more in-depth teaching and instruction.)

What Is "The Spiritual Realm"?

The spiritual realm in Scripture is the "unseen realm" or the "eternal realm:

> *While we look not at the things which are seen, but at the things which are not seen; for the things which are seen are temporal, but the things which are not seen are eternal* (2 Cor. 4:18).

In 2 Kings 6:13–17, we read the account of Elisha praying for his servant's eyes to be opened to "see" into this "unseen realm." It is obvious in this passage that Elisha himself was familiar with this spiritual dimension.

The Scripture clearly describes two kingdoms within the spiritual realm: the kingdom of Satan and the Kingdom of God. In Matthew 12:22–28, Jesus teaches about the reality of these two kingdoms. Colossians 1:12,13 confirms the idea of two kingdoms in the unseen realm. As believers, we are citizens of the Kingdom of Light and this Kingdom cannot be shaken. Glory to God! We are on the winning team!

What Is "The Third Heaven"?

Paul introduces the term "third heaven" in 2 Corinthians 12:2:

> *I know a man in Christ who fourteen years ago—whether in the body I do not know, or out of the body I do not know, God knows—such a man was caught up to the third heaven.*

Genesis 2:1 confirms the idea of a plurality of heavens when it says, *"Thus the **heavens** and the earth were completed, and all their hosts."* Scripture also speaks of the highest heaven: *"Behold, to the LORD your God belong **heaven** and the **highest heavens**"* (Deut. 10:14, emphasis mine).

If the Bible says that there is a "third heaven," the inference then is that there is a first and second heaven as well. It seems that the "first heaven" is the heaven that displays the stars, sun, moon, and earth's atmosphere (see Ps. 8:3). The "second heaven" is believed by many Bible scholars to be the realm from where the demonic hierarchy rules. Daniel 10 describes a wrestling between Jesus (or a high-ranking angel) and the principality of Persia. Apparently, this warfare took place in the second heaven.

Many of today's Christian leaders believe that the third heaven is the throne room of God as described in Revelation 4 and 5, and Isaiah 6. Ephesians 1:20–23 makes it very clear that Christ is seated in the throne room far above all other principalities, powers, names, and titles.

Some enthusiastic "throne zoners" believe there are higher levels than the third heaven and that the third heaven is not necessarily the throne room level. They propose that the third heaven is what Paul refers to as the "Paradise of God" in 2 Corinthians 12:4 and that there are still higher realms beyond. Although this theory could possibly be true, the Bible makes no specific reference to any levels of heaven higher than the third. Any suggestions of higher realms would be "extra-biblical." Although such an idea is not necessarily "anti-biblical," I believe that it is a safeguard to stay within the boundaries of the Scriptures when it comes to "spiritual experience." It is also wisdom!

Ascending and Descending

In Genesis 28:12, we find that Jacob had a dream. In this dream he saw a ladder set up on the earth but the top reached to heaven. Angels were ascending and descending on it. Many on our ministry team have actually experienced the "ascending and descending" dimensions of third-heaven encounters. Is this valid and is it scriptural?

We see Jesus in John 5:19,20 explaining to his disciples that He only did what He saw His Father do. We know through Christ's teaching that *"Our Father... **is in heaven**"* (Matt. 6:9, emphasis mine). It appears that Jesus engaged in encounters with His Father in heaven and then would "download" it into the earthly realm. He only did what He saw His Father do.

Let's look at another example. In Exodus chapters 24–34, we see that Moses ascended to the mountaintop, engaged in divine and heavenly encounters (even ate and drank while beholding God on sapphire streets), and then "descended," bringing the commandments of the Lord to the people. In Chapter 34, we find that even his physical countenance was influenced by the presence of the Lord's glory. As he descended into the camp, His face shone so brilliantly that it had to be veiled to protect the people.

John, Isaiah, and Paul are other Bible characters who also had heavenly visions and encounters and then brought the revelation to the people in the earth. They were "ascending and descending."

Doorway to Heavenly Realms

As discussed earlier in the chapter "New Creation Realities," our spirits were created to enable us to relate to the spirit realm. Our born-again spirits are already familiar with the heavenly dimensions and the realm of the Kingdom of God. We are one with Christ in our spirits. If we understand and believe this reality, it is not too difficult to see how we can enter that spiritual door into divine encounters. It is simply a matter of praying for our souls and bodies to be awakened to spiritual realities.

John, in Revelation 4:1, was given an invitation to enter into the throne room. The Scripture says,

> *and behold, a door standing open in heaven, and the first voice which I had heard, like the sound of a trumpet speaking with me, said, "Come up here, and I will show you what must take place after these things."*

John was shown an open door into heaven and then the voice instructed him to *"Come up here!"* The voice didn't say, "***I*** am going to **bring you up** here." Somehow John had to respond to the command to "come."

Colossians 3:1–2 exhorts us with the following:

> *Therefore if you have been raised up with Christ,* ***keep seeking the things above****, where Christ is, seated at the right hand of God.*
>
> ***Set your mind on the things above****, not on the things that are on earth* (emphasis mine).

Many times, I have heard Christians say, "You can get so heavenly-minded that you are no earthly good." While I understand that this saying most likely addresses those who might be imbalanced (covered in a subsequent chapter), that is not what Colossians 3:1–2 says. This passage actually strongly exhorts us to seek those things above and to set our affections there.

Hebrews 4:16 encourages us to *"draw near with confidence to the throne of grace"* in order to receive mercy, grace, and help in time of need. Where exactly is the throne of grace? Could it be the third heaven? If so, we are urged in the Scripture to "**come boldly**."

Sovereign Act or Faith?

A sovereign act is completely initiated by God Himself and has nothing to do with man's ability, determination, or initiation. It is solely a divine intervention. Often the Lord performs sovereign acts among His people to initiate His purposes. It is like an introduction to what He is about to manifest and establish in the earth.

I believe that the outpouring of the Spirit in the first chapter of Acts is an example of this. Before His ascension, Jesus told His disciples that the promise of the Spirit was coming. They postured themselves in prayer in order to "birth" this promise, but they didn't have a clue what the event was going to look like. The Holy Spirit came in divine timing and by a sovereign move of God. Filled with the Holy Spirit, they all began to speak unknown languages. What a surprise to find each other speaking in these new languages which they had never learned. The believers who had gathered did not *enter into* the experience of speaking in tongues by faith—rather the experience *entered into them.*

There is a difference between the promise of God coming to you and you going to the promise. Sometimes, in prophetic ministry, the Word of God will "come to the prophet," while at other times, the prophet will seek the Lord for the Word.

We can see a similar sovereign principle at work in the area of pastoral ministry. At times the Lord will spontaneously drop the Sunday morning message into the pastor's spirit. The pastor doesn't even need to study it out. The inspiration comes directly to his heart. Most of the time, however, he will need to seek the Lord for the message. He will need to study and access the "message" by faith. One is a sovereign act and the other is by faith. Which one is more valid? Neither. Both are valid. They can both be pure messages from God, but they are received in different ways.

The Scripture does not say that, "the just shall live by sovereign acts." It does state though, *"the just shall live* ***by faith****"* (Rom. 1:17, KJV, emphasis mine). Most believers seldom experience a sovereign act of God. For the average Christian, it is a daily walk of faith through which they access the promises in the Word of God. All the promises have already been secured for us in Christ.

Second Peter 1:3 clearly states,

> *Seeing that His divine power has granted to us everything pertaining to life and godliness, through the true knowledge of Him who called us by His own glory and excellence.*

Ephesians 1:3 similarly states that we have already been *"blessed... with every spiritual blessing in the heavenly places in Christ."* The table of the Lord's blessing has already been set. We simply need to access the promises by faith.

Sometimes individuals actually believe that God will impose His gifts on people. A number of years ago, after I shared the gospel with a woman, she replied in this manner: "If God wants me saved, then He will save me." It was not a question of whether God wanted her saved. He did. He already secured her salvation 2,000 years ago through Christ's death on the cross. His work of salvation would not benefit her, though, unless she accessed it and appropriated it **by faith**. The same is true for all Kingdom promises. Jesus said, *"I came that they may have life, and have it abundantly"* (John 10:10). In John 17:24, Jesus prayed,

> *"Father, I desire that they also, whom You have given Me, be with Me where I am, so that they may see My glory which You have given Me."*

Wow! That sounds like a third-heaven invitation and promise to me. Are we willing to access it by faith? Will the Lord give some individuals a sovereign visitation to the third heaven? Perhaps, but what if we never experience a sovereign encounter? Are we able to visit the glory realms of heaven by faith and still enjoy valid spiritual experiences? What do you think?

Keys to the Heavenly Realm

All of our spiritual experience must be based on the authority of God's Word and His covenant promises. Again, recognize that all the promises and blessings in the Word are ours in Christ.

I would like to see all the "spookiness" removed from "third heaven experience." It is quite simple to understand. Our born-again spirits are already one with heaven. We don't have to "**go**" **anywhere**. We are already there! We are already in the throne room. The Word says we are! If the Word says that we are seated with Christ in the heavenly places, then we are! There is no argument. The Word says it. We believe it. No mysticism. No spooks. No hoping to go. We are just there! Truth says so, whether we feel it or not.

Now, would you like to know how to help your soul and your body become more familiar with what is already real in your spirit? Would you like to know how to "connect" the truth and the reality of heavenly encounters into your emotional, mental, and physical experience? Well then—follow me into the next chapter.

Up, Up, and Away

At the end of this chapter we are going to pray you off into a third heaven journey, but take note: **it is only for those who want to go.**

It is my desire to strip the false perception that godly spiritual experiences are weird, mystical, and dangerous. Spiritual encounters are actually quite normal and natural (and should be, for every believer). However, the language necessary to describe heavenly experiences often tends to make these encounters sound "way out" and unattainable for the average person.

It is God's desire for *everyone* to enjoy spiritual experience. The more you exercise your spirit towards God-encounters, the more natural they become. I believe the teaching that follows will help give you further explanation about being naturally supernatural.

Knowing the Holy Spirit

How well are you acquainted with the Holy Spirit? Are you aware of His presence as you go about your day? Do you listen for His counsel? Are you familiar with what pleases Him and with what displeases Him? The Holy Spirit is committed to leading and guiding us into all truth—but more than anything else, He desires relationship with you. Paul refers to this as "communion with the Spirit" (2 Cor. 13:14). He will teach you all about the third heaven and how to enjoy spiritual experience within the boundaries of the truth. He will never lead you into error.

When you are born again, the Holy Spirit enters your spirit and gives you new life (John 3:6). He is within you right now and within Him are all the gifts and blessings of the Kingdom. In Acts 1:5, Jesus prophesied to His disciples that they would be baptized with the Holy Spirit. The word "baptize" means to be fully immersed or to be completely filled. When you ask the Lord to baptize you in the Spirit, you are actually giving invitation for the Holy Spirit's presence to fill your soul and body, as well as your spirit man where He already resides. In this way, you are completely immersed in Him; this is actually an act of consecration.

It is important to have your soul and body filled with the Spirit when you desire to experience heavenly encounters. Although we must all ask for this infilling the first time, we can also ask for "refills" whenever we need a top-up. Ephesians 5:18 says, *"Be not drunk with wine, wherein is excess; but be filled with the Spirit"* (KJV). The word "filled" here is written in a present, ongoing tense. In other words, it means that you can get filled, and filled, **and filled**! Take time, right now, to get acquainted with the Holy Spirit. He is so lovely. Invite

Him to fill you to overflowing with His holy presence in your body, soul, and spirit. He will!

Now, remember—don't allow your feelings or lack of them to determine if your experience is valid. You are filled because you asked and He answered. The Scripture says so! (See Luke 11:13.)

Sanctified Imagination and Thoughts

Another helpful key to entering into third heaven experience lies within the sanctified imagination and mind. In Ephesians 1:17–18, Paul prays for the Lord to give the believers in Ephesus the spirit of wisdom and revelation in the knowledge of Christ. He also prayed that the *"eyes"* of their *"understanding"* would be enlightened (KJV). The Greek word used here for "understanding" is *dianoia.* It is rendered *"mind,"* *"understanding,"* and *"imagination"* within the Scriptures. Paul is actually praying for the eyes of the imagination or the eyes of the mind to be opened to comprehend supernatural things.

Much of our spiritual revelation is fed into our "image center" (imagination) or our mind. Nonetheless, we are often afraid of using our imagination to receive revelation from the Lord. People at times use the imagination to engage in vain or evil and unclean images, but God never created it to be used this way. The Lord created the imagination as a place within us where He could grant vision, pictures, or images. This is the place where you will often "see" visions of glory. These visions are released from your spirit into your imagination.

God also reveals heavenly glory in your mind by releasing holy and heavenly ideas, counsel, and understanding into your thoughts from your spirit. However, sometimes our minds have been polluted with unclean and ungodly thoughts which defile our mind and distort the accuracy of revelation. It is important to watch over our souls with all diligence.

Many believers are not open to receiving spiritual experience in the imagination or thoughts—yet, that is actually where you will receive most of your spiritual inspirations. If you will allow those "organs of the soul" to be used by the Holy Spirit, you will begin to enjoy more spiritual visions and encounters.

"Practicizing"

Hebrews 5:14 states, *"But strong meat belongeth to them that are of full age, even those who **by reason of use** [practice] have their senses **exercised** to discern both good and evil"* (KJV, emphasis mine). You can "***practicize***" (practice and exercise) your spirit and soul by filling your mind with images and concepts from the Word of God. Read a portion of Scripture, and then picture it in the imagination, then think on it in your thoughts. This will "season" your soul to receive spiritual vision.

You see, the Word of God is spiritual substance. When you submit your imagination and mind to it, the power of that Word (spiritual substance) will fill those very places in the soul to which you are submitting it. "Practicizing" is actually acting on what you believe.

> *Even so faith, if it has no works, is dead, being by itself. But someone may well say, "You have faith*

> *and I have works; show me your faith without the works, and I will show you my faith by my works"* (Jas. 2:17,18).

When you enter into third heaven experience, most of your encounters will take place in your mind and imagination. However, at times your body and emotions will also sense various things.

Avoiding the Pitfalls

Are there possible dangers in this school of spiritual experience? Most definitely **yes**! Any time a person lives outside the perimeters of the Word, way, or will of God in any area of their lives, danger is lurking.

In your natural life, there are things that could be dangerous if you do not abide by proper principles. For example, driving a car can be extremely jeopardous if you do not abide by the laws of the road. Read the owner's manual, abide by the rules, exercise caution, watch out for "the other guy," and you will most likely do great. The inherent dangers of driving should not deter you from getting on that road and heading for your destination.

Here are some examples of dangers that one should be aware of before getting in the "driver's seat" of spiritual experience:

1. Witchcraft and Occultism

Any activity or manipulation of the spirit realm not under the rule of Christ is called witchcraft. This practice is forbidden in Scripture. Be careful of "guided imagery," a practice in which someone else tells you what to see—this can lead to manipulation (see Deut. 18:10–14; Gal. 5:17–25).

2. Idolatry and Unhealthy Fascination

Our passion must always be for the Lord Himself first and we must be careful to always place Him at the center of our affections. We must avoid being overly fascinated with spiritual experience. John, in Revelation 19:10, had fallen into deception when he began to worship the angel that brought him the vision. John was the closest to Jesus' heart and yet even **he** was in danger of deception. Beware.

3. Experience Orientation

When believers focus too much on spiritual experiences, they can begin to believe that the experiences are the endorsements of their character and maturity. This is not the case. Love, true worship of Christ, as well as faith and obedience to the Word of God are the real hallmarks of authentic Christian living.

4. Pride and Self-Exaltation

No one is exempt from pride. Lucifer himself, even though he was the covering cherub over the ark and a high-ranking angel in heaven, fell into the sin of pride. That sin cost Lucifer his place in heaven. He was cast out! The Apostle Peter is a classic example of how pride and self rule can begin to rise up even right in the midst of divine encounter. While on the Mount of Transfiguration, he said, *"Lord, it is good for us to be here"* and arrogantly told Jesus what they should be doing (see Matt. 17:1–8). Paul was also aware that he was susceptible to pride because of the "abundance of revelations" (see 2 Cor. 12:1–7). If even these Bible figures could fall, it is vital that we guard against pride. A good accountability team will often help. Remember, pride is a deception—you cannot usually see it yourself. Listen to others!

5. Touched But Not Changed

Christ's ministry touched Israel for over three years. He ministered powerfully, healing the sick, cleansing the lepers, raising the dead, and liberating the oppressed. Many were powerfully touched and yet at the end of Christ's ministry with them He wept, saying,

> *"If you had known in this day, even you, the things which make for peace!... You did not recognize the time of your visitation"* (Luke 19:42,44).

The nation had been powerfully visited by the manifested "dunamis" of God, and yet those who gathered in His final hour cried, *"Crucify Him!"* All His disciples had fled. Peter denied Him. Judas betrayed Him. They were touched but not changed.

In the renewal movement that broke forth into the nations through the Toronto outpouring in 1994, the Lord graciously and gloriously ministered to the multitudes, yet many were not transformed. When you receive a powerful touch from the Lord's hand, it says nothing about you. It doesn't endorse *your* character or *your* ministry. It does, however, say something about the Lord. It says He is mighty! He is loving and merciful!

If I were to lavishly give a million dollars to a friend, the gesture says nothing about her. It does say something though, about me—perhaps that I am generous. We will learn something about my friend, however, once she does something with the money. If she uses the gift to build homes for the homeless, that says something about her. If she sets up a prostitution ring, that says something about her, too. The manifested goodness of the Lord is to bring blessing, repentance, and enrichment to our lives, but there are no guarantees—our response to His acts of kindness is the determining factor. Heavenly encounters have the potential to enrich and empower a believer's walk. May we be touched *and* changed!

6. Error and Deception

Entering into spiritual experience without a proper and complete foundation in the Word of God can sometimes open the door to error and deception. Good solid Bible teaching should always accompany spiritual experience. If you see a vision or enjoy an encounter in the glory realm, then study it out in the Word of God afterwards. **Always** let the Word of God be the first testing place to validate experience!

Here We Go!

Are you ready? Read along and respond as we go through a "pre-trip check-up."

1. Are You Born Again?

If not, give your heart to Jesus right now. Invite Him, in simple words, to come into your life and forgive your sins. He will!

2. Renounce Past New Age and Occult Practices

We serve one God and **one God only**! All other gods and spiritual practices outside the perimeters of biblical instruction must be renounced. Repent for your involvement in spiritual activities that have been forbidden in the Scriptures (see Deut. 18:10–14). Ask the Lord to forgive you and to cleanse your life according to 1 John 1:9.

3. Pray That Your Spirit, Soul, and Body Be Sanctified

Invite the Holy Spirit to fill you afresh and to set apart your spirit, body, and soul (including your mind, will, emotions, and imagination) for heavenly and divine encounters.

4. Focus on Jesus

Begin to worship and adore Him. Set your mind and your affections on Him and on those things above where He is seated.

5. Believe That You "Are There"

The Scripture says that you are in the throne room. Believe it.

6. Drink

Begin to drink of the glory of the heavenly realm by faith.

7. Open Your Spiritual "Eyes" to See

Be open to receiving vision or experience in your imagination, mind, emotions, and body. Take note of anything that you are seeing or sensing. If it is dim or weak, continue to lean into it. It will usually get stronger. Record what you experience and then study it out through the Scripture following your encounter. Invite the Holy Spirit to teach you more about the encounter.

8. THANK HIM

Thank the Lord for the wonderful encounter with Him and believe Him for MORE!

Pray the following prayer with me as we get ready to receive spiritual encounters:

Heavenly Father, thank You for allowing me bold access into the throne room. Thank You for creating in me a spirit that is able to relate to the spirit realm. I invite you to grant me rich and meaningful spiritual experience in Your presence so that my walk with You and my mission in the earth might be enriched.

I submit myself to You, Holy Spirit, and will follow You into glorious experiences in the Kingdom. I release my heart to You now. Fill me please with Your glory! Draw me into intimacy with You and give me an awareness of my position with You in the heavenly places. In Jesus' Name. AMEN.

Now, focus on Him, the heavenly realm, His glory... and enjoy. If you sense nothing at all—remember, your spirit is engaged in divine encounters even if your "soul" is not aware of the experience. Remain in faith and thanksgiving. Blessings!

Up, Up, and Away!

Colors, Rainbows, and Glory Clouds

While caught up in worship during a Sunday morning service, I became aware of being enveloped in the color purple. The color in this closed-eye vision was deep, rich, and penetrating. Our ministry teams, in their "third heaven journeys," have found that colors are actually spiritual substance which carry prophetic meaning. For example, purple represents royalty and authority.

Color imagery is found throughout the Bible. Priestly garments are associated with colors like purple, scarlet, blue, and gold. To find prophetic qualities associated with certain colors, you simply look up the colors in a Bible concordance. Proceed to examine the Scriptures referencing the colors to discover their common usage. For example, the color green in the Bible is often found in the context of trees, leaves, and grass. These things speak of growth and renewal. The leaves mentioned in Ezekiel and Revelation are found in the context of healing. The man mentioned in Psalm 1 was like a tree planted by rivers of living water—his leaves would not wither and whatever he put his hand to prospered. When you examine the imagery for the color green in Scripture, you can deduce that the prophetic qualities could be those of renewal, growth, healing, and prosperity.

In the Rainbow

When you see colors in the spirit, it is possible by faith to receive the spiritual essence of the prophetic quality they represent. For instance, in the "purple" worship experience that I just related, I felt the Holy Spirit encourage me to soak in the color that I was seeing in this vision—as I did so, I would imbibe of the Lord's royal authority and majesty. The Scripture says in Matthew 28:18–20, that all authority in the heavens and in the earth has been given to Jesus and that we are to go in this authority to disciple the nations. By faith, I responded to the Holy Spirit's unction and began to enjoy soaking in the color purple. I drank deep of Christ's royal authority and sensed an infilling taking place.

While enjoying the color purple, a new hue began to appear. In my vision I could now see the essence of the color blue enveloping me in the same way the purple had. Blue is the color that represents revelation, the prophetic, God's faithfulness, and open heaven. I was delighted to find myself immersed in this color. This experience may sound "out of this world" (it was), but it was also spiritually enriching and fun.

After a few moments in "prophetic blue," I realized I was gazing into green. Then it dawned on me: *Oh my—I am in the rainbow over the throne!* (See Ezek.

1:26–28 and Rev. 4:3.) I exploded into ecstatic worship and praise. Oh, how good God is! The rainbow represents covenant and the colors represent various dimensions of the Lord's glory and goodness.

You will notice that often colors have an influence on our soul. For example, the color brown might leave one feeling very subdued (or bored), while the color orange might impart an energetic feeling. Behavioral scientists have discovered that colors like yellow and orange will often stimulate the appetite, while the color pink has a peaceful and restful influence on people. For this reason, many restaurant owners use orange and yellow in their decor, and prison administrators have sometimes chosen to paint the interiors of their institutions pink.

Some colors of the glory realm are absolutely indescribable! Everything created by God's word is full of "spirit" and "life." Colors are no exception. God is the One who created colors. They are part of God's heavenly glory and Kingdom and the Lord does use them to communicate heavenly revelation to us. I am so glad that the Lord created color. It adds vibrancy and flair to life and is given to us by God to enjoy (see John 6:63).

Christians are sometimes afraid of exploring the prophetic value of color due to the way the New Age movement has misused "colors" in its spiritual encounters. They are not to be worshiped or to be used outside of relationship with Christ as omens or for divination. Don't ever forget that Satan is a "copy cat." Some New Age practitioners have manipulated the spiritual "energy" of colors and—to some degree—even worshiped them. They use colors to divine, to read a person's mood by "seeing" their "aura," and to release a supernatural "healing" through the manipulation of color energy fields.

Scripture is clear—any manipulation of the spirit realm outside of complete submission to Christ's authority and leading is called witchcraft and is a forbidden and illegal practice. Jesus is the God of all spirits and He alone is to be looked to for spiritual encounters and experiences.

New Age practitioners are violating God's boundaries if they manipulate and operate in spiritual energy under the rule of their own soul. We as Christians, however, are under Christ's authority and rule. We follow the leading of the Holy Spirit. The third heaven and all of its glory and authority belongs to us who are "in Christ." The authority of this realm does not belong to those outside of Christ.

Father of Lights

At times, colors will be seen as shimmering lights. Our ministry has received numerous testimonies from believers who have entered the third heaven realm and have seen colored lights permeating heaven's atmosphere. Others have testified to seeing these colored lights in the earthly realm through their spiritual vision.

James 1:17 gives us insights into these lights:

> *Every good thing given and every perfect gift is from above, coming down from the* ***Father of lights****, with whom there is no variation or shifting shadow* (emphasis mine).

We can sometimes see the reflection of the heavenly lights and colors manifested in our experience. I believe these come from the "Father of lights" and represent dimensions of His character, nature, and gifts. At times, angels are seen as colored lights (to be covered later).

A few years ago, our ministry took a team across Canada. We were traveling through northern Ontario late one evening following a meeting, on our way to where we were to stay. We were some distance from the city and the sky was very dark. Suddenly, the northern lights appeared in a glorious display of their radiance. The entire sky was filled with their dancing performance. I had a strong sense that this phenomenon could be a spiritual display of glory from the Father of Lights, perhaps even with angelic involvement. Scientists have some theories regarding the northern lights but, from what I understand, they have yet to discover the exact source of the phenomenon.

Colors can also represent diversities of anointing and gifting. One Sunday while in our local church service, I received a very powerful visitation of the Lord accompanied by a vision in which I saw a "coat of many colors" made up of brilliant, colored lights. The colors in this particular vision represented a multifaceted anointing and gifting that the Lord was going to release, by His "dunamis power," through our local church and apostolic center.

Glory Clouds and Mists

In Exodus 33, we find Moses entering the tent of meeting to spend time with God. The Scripture states that **every** time he entered the tent, *"the pillar of cloud* *would descend"* (see v. 9). As the glory of God visited Moses, from the cloud, the Lord would speak to him face to face. In Scripture, the glory cloud is a **sign of the Lord's presence**—when it manifests, open your ears to hear from the Lord.

The glory cloud also **brings direction**. The cloud of the Lord's presence led Israel during their journey through the wilderness. When it was time for them to move on, the cloud would move and they were to follow.

The Lord will sometimes **release ministry calls** out of the glory cloud. We find, in Exodus 24:16–18, that Moses was called by the Lord out of the *"midst of the cloud"* (v. 16) to stand in the Lord's presence for 40 days and 40 nights. During this time God gave him the pattern for building the tabernacle. At that time, God also gave Moses the Ten Commandments. The Lord will often release new calls into our lives when the glory cloud visits us. At times He will also **grant visions and strategies** for the advancement of His Kingdom.

In Exodus 14, the glory cloud was also a **protection** for Israel against its enemies. The Lord actually caused the pillar of cloud to come between the Egyptian army and the camp of Israel. Later in the story, the Lord looked down on the Egyptians through the cloud, created confusion among them, and caused their chariots to swerve out of control.

In Isaiah 58:8, Scripture confirms that the glory of the Lord is our rear guard. In our ministry we have noticed that at times when there is strong warfare around us, one of our most powerful weapons is to invite an increase of glory to cover us. It is very effective. The enemy cannot penetrate that cloud of glory.

The glory cloud also **ministers discipline**. In Matthew 17:5 we find that *"a bright cloud overshadowed"* Peter, James, and John. The Lord then spoke out of the cloud bringing their focus completely back onto Jesus. This brought adjustment to Peter's behavior (as we pointed out earlier).

In some meetings, I have seen a "mist" hovering over an area of a room. I am aware, at those times, that the Spirit is doing a work in the people in that section. I will often ask the Lord how He wants me to cooperate with His Spirit. Sometimes, I will sense to move prophetically over folks within that section. At other times, I will simply describe what I "see" and invite the people to receive the touch of the Lord's presence. During some ministry calls where the glory mist has been evident, almost entire seating sections of believers go down under the Holy Spirit's power.

In some experiences, the glory mist is colored. I can remember seeing a greenish-colored mist hovering over a particular person in a meeting. This was a sign to me that the Lord was ministering health, renewal, and prosperity to that individual. I simply declared those blessings over her and invited her to receive this divine outpouring on her life. This grateful believer began to drink in God's goodness and soon experienced refreshment, renewal, and hope.

As we discussed in chapter 7, we can train our spiritual senses to become more acute so that we can "see" the glory, the colors, the rainbows and other manifestations of the Kingdom of God. Our heavenly Father reveals these aspects of the glory realm to bring us into a deeper, fuller relationship with Himself and His Kingdom. With every encounter, the Lord wants to inspire us to worship and commune with Him. Invite Him to teach and mentor you in the glories of the heavenly realm. You are a Kingdom child and these experiential blessings are your portion as a "citizen" of heaven (Eph. 2:19). Colors, rainbows, and glory clouds—they are yours in Him!

Fire, Fire Alarms, and Firemen

"What is that smell?" asked one of the intercessors with alarm in her voice. "It smells like smoke," replied another. *Uh-oh, did I leave something on the stove with the burner on?* I wondered.

My memory quickly took me back to 1980, when Ron and I and our children lived in a Christian community house for a few months while waiting to go to Bible school. A close friend, Sharon Clark, also lived in that community and was assigned to cooking meals for the team we lived with. I helped her at times. We would often sneak outside in the fresh spring air for times of worship in the midst of a meal-prep assignment. The beautiful country setting inspired us to worship and pray. We justified our "time out" from duty due to the fact that the beans would take at least a couple of hours until they were fully cooked—that should give us plenty of time to worship, pray, enjoy the Lord and get back in time to put the meal on the table.

Time and time again, though, we would become enraptured in God's presence and forget our earthly and "mundane" responsibilities. We would be abruptly jarred out of "hallelujah la-la land" by the loud shriek of the fire alarm! Oh, no—in trouble again! Quickly running back to the kitchen, we would find the beans, or the bread, or the stew, or whatever else we were cooking, burned to a crisp at the bottom of the pan and the kitchen filled with clouds of smoke (and believe me, this was *not* "holy smoke"). After a number of these occurrences, the leaders of our community found it necessary to discipline us and to sternly exhort us to keep focused—after all, we could burn the house down!

"What's that smell?"

This vivid memory of the wailing fire alarm faded and I was back in our intercession meeting. With visions of burning beans, I raced to the kitchen. *Phew!* All was well. Praise God, I hadn't left a burner on; but, what *was* that smell? The aroma of fire got stronger. Everyone in the prayer meeting began to run through the house, searching for the source. The search proved fruitless and so we ran outdoors thinking that perhaps the outside of our house was on fire. Yet, again we found no evidence. When we met back in the living room, the odor of smoke was increasing but there was still no evidence of flames anywhere.

Though very puzzled, we continued our prayer meeting, interceding for a five-night revival event in our city called "***Wind and Fire***." Minutes later, we were shaken from our prayers as a fire engine, with siren blaring, screamed down our street. "Aha! There *is* a fire," I wittingly concluded.

Running After the Fire Truck

We decided to follow the fire truck down the street where we saw the firemen scurrying around looking confused. I inquired, "Is there a fire in our neighborhood?" The fireman answered, "We received an urgent call that there was a house on fire on Badger Avenue, but we cannot seem to find evidence of any fire at all." He concluded that it must have been a false alarm.

When we returned to prayer, we did "wonder" what this fire, fire alarm, and visitation of firemen was all about. We had been previously praying for the Lord to visit us with signs and wonders. With sudden insight, one of the intercessors said, "Hey, I know what this is. It's a "wonder"—we wonder what it is!" "O.K, whatever!" we replied.

We became increasingly convinced that we had experienced a "heavenly wonder." Acts 2:19 says,

> *"And I will grant* ***wonders*** *in the sky above and* ***signs*** *on the earth below, blood, and* ***fire****, and vapor of* ***smoke"*** (emphasis mine).

This was our first introduction to some of the manifestations of the glory realm that we were about to witness in weeks to come. The five days of scheduled meetings turned into 21 days and nights of a glorious outpouring of the Spirit of God in our city. We enjoyed "the wind and fire" of the Holy Spirit's presence. We delighted in signs, wonders, and miracles. We rejoiced over salvations, baptisms, healings, and deliverances in people's lives. We stood in awe, night after night, over the signs we witnessed: the appearance of angels in the meetings and in the sky over the city, the visitation of the fragrances of the Lord's presence, and so many other types of divine blessings.

Check for Fire!

One evening, the entire conference center was filled with a strong smell of fire. The janitor frantically checked all the alarms and every room for the source of this mysterious phenomenon. Most of those present were also aware of the odor. There were times when a smoky mist seemed to hover over the meeting. Isaiah 6:4 recounts a similar experience. During Isaiah's visitation to the throne room, he saw the temple "filling with smoke."

After thoroughly checking the building, we realized we were experiencing a heavenly and divine visitation of the "fire of God." These experiences raise the questions: What is the fire of God, and what is its purpose? Let's see what Scripture says.

Baptized with Fire

In Matthew 3 we see evidence of three baptisms. The first baptism with water, a sign of repentance, was officiated by John the Baptist. The next two baptisms were prophesied by John in verses 11 and 12:

> *"As for me, I baptize you with water for repentance, but He who is coming after me is mightier than I, and I am not fit to remove His sandals;* ***He will baptize you with the Holy Spirit and fire.*** *His winnowing fork is in His hand, and He will thoroughly clear His threshing floor; and He will gather His wheat into the barn, but He will burn up the chaff with unquenchable fire"* (emphasis mine).

The Lord has a plan to completely immerse and fill us (baptize us) with His fire. On the day of Pentecost in Acts 2, Scripture records a corporate outpouring and baptism of the Holy Spirit which empowered believers to witness for Christ. This is the main ingredient necessary for advancing the Kingdom of God. "Tongues of fire" "rested" on the believers, but there is no actual evidence of "baptism" (full immersion and filling) of the fire. It is my belief that the corporate baptism of fire is yet to come, even though individual believers can always access the blessing of the fire of God at any time by faith.

The baptism with fire, at the end of the Church age, will "burn the dross" and impurities from Christ's Body, the Church. Through this work of grace, the glorious Church will be revealed in the earth. The burning up of the impurities will then allow the manifestation of the radiant glory and brilliance of the Church.

Fire that Refines

Isaiah prophesied, *"Arise, shine; for your light has come, And the glory of the LORD has risen upon you"* (Isa. 60:1). He further prophesies in this chapter that the manifested glory will actually be seen upon the people of God and will result in kings and entire nations coming to the glory of Christ. The word "light" in verse one refers to "illumination that comes from fire." This could be referring to a corporate "baptism with fire" which will cause the glory to be displayed visibly through God's people to the nations of the earth.

Malachi alludes to this in chapter 3:1–4, where he declares that the Lord will suddenly come to His temple as a refiner's fire. He will purge the priesthood so that they will bring holy offerings to Him.

Consuming Fire

The Book of Hebrews also refers to God's fiery nature. *"Our God is a consuming fire"* (Heb. 12:29). The Lord not only refines with His fire, but He consumes. What does He consume? Deuteronomy 9:3 says that He consumes and devours His enemies. Malachi suggests in chapter 4:1–3 that He consumes the proud and the arrogant.

Fire of Protection

Zechariah 2:5 speaks of the fire of God as a protective wall around Zion and that the Lord's glory is in the midst of her. When His fire is around us, the enemy cannot come near. The fire protects.

Fire of Consecration

In Isaiah chapter 6, the prophet experiences burning as a coal from the altar is placed on his lips. This fire experience purges him of his uncleanness and takes him to a new level of consecration to empower his prophetic ministry.

Fire of Love and Passion

The Book of Revelation vividly describes Jesus as one whose *"eyes were like a flame of fire"* (Rev. 1:14). I believe this fire in His eyes to be the pure passion of His love towards us. Song of Solomon 8:6,7 extols this passion, the strength of love's flame: "Many waters cannot quench it."

Healing Fire

Malachi 4:1–3 further extends the fire imagery, describing Jesus as the "Sun" of righteousness. What is the sun? It is a ball of fire. Jesus is like a righteous fire. When Jesus manifests as the "Sun of righteousness" there is healing in His wings.

It is believed that the "wings" refer to the jets of gaseous flames that exude from the sun. In the "wings" of His fire, people can find healing. On occasion, some of our ministry associates have witnessed the fire of God literally burning out cancer and other diseases. In addition, people often testify to feeling a burning of fire in the area where they were afflicted.

Fire that Bears Witness

On the road to Emmaus, the disciples actually experienced a burning within when the presence of the Lord was with them. Even King David, in Psalm 39:3, experienced this fire: *"My heart was hot within me, While I was musing the fire burned; Then I spoke with my tongue."*

At times, in the presence of the Lord you can also actually "feel" a strong burning within your spirit. This is not "heartburn" or a menopausal "hot flash." No, this is the fire of God that is bearing witness of the manifestation of the Lord's presence.

THE FIRE'S GLORIOUS WORK

The fire of God accomplishes many things. It is good to experience the fire and its glorious work. Our ministry team know of many who have seen the flames and the fire of God in visionary or spiritual experiences. Every experience is different. Fire is also seen in heaven around the altar of prayer and intercession (see Rev. 8:5). God's ministers are referred to as flames of fire (Ps. 104:4).

Once during a third-heaven encounter, I saw myself before the throne of God, being transformed into a flame of fire. God was igniting me spiritually for a fresh assignment in ministry.

Fire Is a Covenant Blessing

The fire is a covenant blessing for all covenant children. Would you like it to blaze within your life? You can have it—it is yours by faith! Posture yourself to receive and remember that faith is not hope—*"faith is the assurance of things hoped for, the conviction of things not seen"* (Heb. 11:1). Receive the fire by faith and believe that it is performing its glorious work within you. *Be a blazing fire for Him!*

Honkin' Big Angels and Chariot Rides

"AHHHHHHHHH" I screamed, in absolute terror! It's not every day you see a 20 foot angel hanging out in your living room. *Yikes!*

A group of us were engaged in intercession in our home. As I looked up from prayer, I saw an open vision of this heavenly creature. We were gathered in the living room, a two-story open section of our home overlooked by a dining area on the second-floor balcony. The angel was standing, with its torso filling the entire upper level of the room. The top of its head went through the ceiling. I was able to see one of its wings stretched out over the living room and through the wall to the outside of the house. The span of the wing must have been about 20 feet and its height was about 6 feet. The actual height of the angel could have been well over 20 feet. (This is a *big* creature. However, in another encounter a few years later, I actually saw an angel that filled the entire sky above the horizon.) Now I ask you, wouldn't you scream if *you* saw such a creature? No wonder the angels in the Bible regularly encouraged those they visited to "fear not."

Unfortunately, as soon as I screamed, I lost vision of the angel—this saddened me. (Sometimes, our responses in the natural realm jar our sensitivity to the spiritual realm.) I did, however, feel a holy presence in our home for about three days following the vision.

I began to ask the Lord why He had granted this sovereign angelic visitation. Our ministry had been in a season of very strong assault from a demonic principality and it seemed as though this angel was ministering assurance to us. Angels are on assignment and one of their functions is *"to minister for them who shall be heirs of salvation"* (Heb. 1:14, KJV). Angels' assignments vary as to the need of the believer, but this one definitely gave us a sense of security and protection. Following that time, the warfare seemed to wane and breakthroughs came.

Angels from the Resource Department in Heaven

A number of years ago, our core team was interceding for a ministry assignment the Lord had given us. To fulfill this assignment, we required a large amount of finance and level of faith far beyond anywhere we had been before. During that prayer meeting, I saw a vision of what appeared to be the "resource department of heaven." I saw gold, silver, and commodities of every sort. The Lord declares in

Scripture, *"The silver is Mine and the gold is Mine"* (Haggai 2:8). The Word also assures us that *"God will supply all your needs according to His riches in glory in Christ Jesus"* (Phil. 4:19).

There is provision stored up for God's covenant children that will enable us to feed and clothe the needy of the world. During my glimpse into heaven that day, the Lord showed me that He was going to dispatch angels from the resource department in heaven to serve our ministry. These angelic ministers would bring in the provision needed to fulfill every assignment that He would place in our hands. Since that time, we have repeatedly witnessed miraculous provision that has enabled us to fulfill Kingdom mandates.

Seraphim

In Isaiah 6, we find the prophet engaged in a "throne zone" experience. In the throne room we find a particular type of angel called "seraphim." Angels are different in appearance and in function. *Seraphim* means "fiery ones." It is my belief that these angelic beings minister holiness and the purging that comes from fire. It is possible that these beings are even made up of fire. The ministry of these angels purged Isaiah's iniquity and prepared him for his next assignment.

Cherubim

God gave Isaiah a vision of seraphim while, for Ezekiel, He gave a vision of the cherubim. The *cherubim* guarded the tree of life in Genesis 3:24. Later, God instructed Moses to place golden cherubim over the mercy seat (Ex. 25).

The book of Ezekiel describes the unusual and awesome appearance of the cherubim and makes it clear that they are stewards of the glory. Cherubim ushered the glory into the temple and removed it when Israel was unrepentant (see Ezek. 1–10). When the glory of the Lord manifests in meetings, you can often sense the presence of angels as well. Angels usher in the glory.

Zoa (Living Creatures)

In Revelation 4:6, we find reference to the living creatures around the throne. They are full of eyes in front and behind (as also are the wheels of the cherubim). This is interesting to note, as eyes are the organ that allows us to "see." These creatures carry a powerful revelation of Jesus as they see various dimensions of His nature and character. They cry "Holy, holy, holy" day and night. In a throne room visitation, it is possible to see these creatures—John did.

Chariots and Chariot Drivers

The heavenly realm is full of innumerable surprises for us. Have you ever imagined what it would be like to ride in a chariot pulled by angels? While in a revival meeting on Vancouver Island a number of years ago, I strongly discerned the presence of angels. While I continued to ponder this, the evangelist began to declare, "There is a lot of angelic activity here tonight." *Wow!* It is always encouraging to receive confirmation of a discernment. Those in the crowd who were discerning angels were invited to come forward. A number of us responded. The evangelist then invited the Lord to dispatch the angels to perform whatever they were called to do.

Immediately, I found myself sitting in a chariot. I had gone into a trance-type of vision, but what was amazing was that I could actually *feel* the seat of the chariot under me. I was aware of darkness all around. I then found myself suddenly being pulled by a team of angels, who were about to take me for the ride of my life!

I heard them laughing uproariously as they whipped me around corners and drew me up, down, and around at breakneck speed, on what seemed like a roller-coaster track. I gripped tightly on to the side of the chariot while literally feeling a wind blowing across my face. Even though the ride was extremely thrilling, I was still "freaked out," because I couldn't see where we were going. In spite of my uneasiness, the angels certainly appeared to enjoy themselves.

I believe that I was in the vision for approximately ten minutes. When I came out of the vision, I asked of the Lord what the purpose of this little excursion was. His answer was simple: *"I just wanted you to have fun."* Really? You mean, God is "into" *fun*?

God actually delights in being playful with His children. Perhaps we get too intense and serious at times. The Lord often has special little surprises along the way that minister refreshment to us. The Word confirms that angelic chariots, chariot drivers, and even spirit horses are for real—they truly are! (See 2 Kings 11,12; 6:13–17; Zech. 1:8–11; Ps. 68:7.)

Chief Princes

Angels not only have different functions, forms, and shapes, but they vary in rank and position as well.

Lucifer, for example, was a high-ranking angel in heaven before he fell.*

Chief princes or archangels are given jurisdiction over land and special events. Michael is referred to in the Scriptures as an *archangel* or chief prince (see Jude 1:9 and Dan. 10:13). It is believed that Michael oversees warfare and is the chief prince over the affairs of Israel.

Not long ago, at a national prayer assembly in Canada, a prophet had a vision that seems to confirm this role of Michael. Following three days of identificational repentance, this respected prophet saw a vision of the archangel Michael leading an entourage of angels from Israel to Canada. At the time, we had been humbling ourselves before God in repentance for our sinful choices as a nation towards Israel. An historical work of reconciliation took place at that meeting and since that time, Canada has seen the fruit of it.

Like Michael, the angel Gabriel is also believed to be an archangel. Many prophetic people sense that this high-ranking angel is in charge of communication and

---

**One can actually be in the very presence of God and still choose to sin. Some spiritually enthusiastic Christians tend to believe that their spiritual encounters and numerous experiences in the glory realm are a sign and endorsement of their spiritual maturity. This is far from true. Lucifer couldn't have been any closer to the glory and yet he chose to sin.*

Peter while in the midst of a divine encounter on the Mount of Transfiguration, fell into pride. John the Beloved, during an apocalyptic vision and encounter with an angel, was tempted to enter worship of the angel. A believer's maturity in Christ is based upon the choices of the heart. It is these choices that determine the character and maturity level of a child of God.

special messages. In Scripture, Gabriel always seemed to be involved when momentous messages were to be heralded. In recent years I have heard many testimonies from believers who have been visited by angels bringing them messages from the throne room.

Common Angels

The Scriptures also clearly teach that angels encamp around the righteous—we are surrounded! We have come to an *"innumerable company of angels,"* the writer of Hebrews declares (see Heb. 12:22, KJV). These angels often minister the purposes and nature of the Lord to us. For example, "spirits of wisdom" minister the wisdom of the Kingdom to us. "Spirits of revelation" minister the revelation of Christ, while "spirits of grace" minister His favor. God gives each angel a different assignment.

Colored Angels?

We have witnessed angels which radiate color. In Australia, a number of us fellowshipped in a restaurant following a meeting. In the corner of the room I saw a bright green mist. At the time, I was not very familiar with the angelic realm but there was an internationally renowned prophetic minister with us who was very acquainted with angels and their activity. She confidently interjected, "Oh, that is a renewal angel and it is here to minister healing and revival." She said that if any of us were interested in receiving renewal and healing, we should go and stand in the area where the green mist lingered.

Well, I was into *that,* for sure! About half a dozen of us quickly charged to the corner of the room to stand in the presence of this angelic presence. While in our huddle, laughing, rejoicing and doing a few "crunchies," our waitress walked into our private room in the restaurant. She didn't know what to think and looked a bit shocked. One of the guests attempted to comfort her, saying, "Oh, they're fine—they're just seeing an angel." The waitress seemed a bit stunned. I do believe, though, that she was extremely blessed following our departure from the restaurant to find that we had tipped her with an enormously extravagant tip. *Hmmm—maybe angel lovers aren't so bad after all.*

Increased Awareness of the Angelic

Today, the Body of Christ is becoming increasingly aware of angelic activity. This is a good sign. All throughout the Scriptures we see evidence of angels and their interaction with man.

Whether you sense them or not, angels are all around you—the Word says so! They are wonderful creatures sent to minister the love, grace, and glory of the Lord and His Kingdom. As Elisha prayed for the eyes of his servant to be opened to see angels, so also I pray for you. Enjoy!

Portals of Glory

In February 2002, I received a vision in which I saw "portals of glory" opening in heaven. In the vision, rays of glory beamed down out of the heavens into various places on earth. As we discovered in a previous chapter, the glory of God represents His abundance, riches, weight of His presence, splendor, and goodness. The glory can manifest in many different ways, but it is always a demonstration of the Father's lovingkindness.

Portals are points of entry. A portal could be a gate, a door, or a window. Psalm 24:7 says, *"Lift up your heads, O* ***gates****, And be lifted up, O ancient* ***doors****, That the King of glory may come in!"* (emphasis mine). The gates or doors here could be also called "portals" or openings. This particular portion of Scripture indicates that when the portals are opened, the King of glory will come in.

Genesis 28 suggests that portals can be found in specific geographical regions. Jacob saw in a dream an opening into the heavens into which angels were ascending and from which they were descending:

> *Then Jacob departed from Beersheba and went toward Haran. He came to* ***a certain place*** *and spent the night there, because the sun had set; and he took one of the stones of* ***the place*** *and put it under his head, and lay down in that place. He had a dream, and behold, a ladder was set on the earth with its top reaching to heaven; and behold, the angels of God were ascending and descending on it* (Gen. 28:10–12, emphasis mine).

God seems to grace some geographical locations with specific anointings, outpourings, and manifestations. Perhaps portals of glory are opened up over those regions. This possibly explains what happened in Toronto when the outpouring of the Spirit began in 1994. God poured out great blessing and power in that specific place and then it spilled out to every continent. Most people who attended the renewal meetings in Toronto during the outpouring can testify of visitations of the Lord's power on people in restaurants, elevators, hallways, hotel rooms, streets, at hot dog stands as well as in the conference center.

Another scriptural example of a geographical "portal of glory" was Bethesda (see John 5:2–4). A pool of water in Bethesda was visited periodically by an angel who would stir the waters. The first one who entered the pool received healing.

In Psalm 24 we read that we are to open the gates so that the King of glory may come forth. There are ways that we can open the gates (portals) of glory over our lives and even geographical territories of land. Opening portals produces an "open heaven."

The Open Heaven

The following are some of the open heaven blessings that sometimes manifest through portals of glory:

1. Prosperity

When the heavens are open over your life, everything prospers around you and all the works of your hands are blessed (see Deut. 28:12; Mal. 3:11).

2. Visions

Ezekiel and John both experienced visions when the heavens were opened. Often an open heaven will increase sensitivity to dreams and visions (see Ezek.1:1; Rev. 4:1).

3. Visitations of the Holy Spirit

Following Jesus' baptism, *"the heavens were opened unto him"* (Matt. 3:16, KJV) and the Spirit of God descended upon Him in the form of a dove. Jesus was empowered by the Spirit for His earthly ministry which included demonstrations of healing, deliverance, raising the dead, cleansing lepers, and numerous miracles, signs and wonders. Scripture says that *"the heavens were opened unto him."* The heavens can open over any individual who is correctly postured before God (see Matt. 3:16; Acts 10:38).

4. Victory in Warfare

Jesus is the King of Glory, The Lord of Hosts, the Lord mighty in battle. When the portals of heaven are opened, Jesus, along with His armies in heaven, is released to wage war with righteousness and justice (see Ps. 24; Rev. 19:11–17).

5. Angelic Visitations

Jacob's dream is evidence that when the heavens are opened, angels ascend and descend (see also John 1:51).

How to Open the Heavens

It is possible for us to posture ourselves to receive the benefits of the open heaven. The blessings of heaven cannot be earned, for they have been freely given to us in Christ (see Eph. 1:3), but we can position ourselves to receive them (like a child reaching out hands to accept a gift). The following are some things that we can do to posture ourselves to receive.

1. Repentance

In Matthew 3, John the Baptist preaches a message of repentance and baptizes in water. When Jesus approaches him for baptism, John resists the idea. John says, *"I have need to be baptized by You, and do You come to me?"* (Matt. 3:14). He knew that Jesus had never sinned. In John's mind, this baptism was for sinners—not for Jesus, the Righteous.

Christ answers John's objection: *"Permit it at this time; for in this way it is fitting for us to fulfill all righteousness"* (Matt. 3:15). I believe that Jesus was actually entering here into repentance for all mankind. Christ, and Christ alone, was to fulfill all the requirements that God had set for man to come into everlasting relationship with Him. What was the result of Jesus' obedience in baptism? In verse 16 we read,

> *After being baptized, Jesus came up immediately from the water; and behold,* ***the heavens were opened,***

and he saw the ***Spirit of God descending as a dove and lighting on Him*** (emphasis mine).

From that point on, Jesus ministered in the power of the Spirit with miracles, signs, and wonders accompanying the preaching of the Word. He ministered under an open heaven and the entire nation was influenced as a result.

Another example of repentance leading to an open heaven can be found in the book of Daniel. God's people were under Babylonian oppression and control due to their sin and idolatry. If you serve sin, you will surely become a slave of sin (see Rom. 6:16). The people of God were paying a heavy penalty for their compromise.

In Chapter 9, Daniel confessed his sins and the sins of his people, requesting forgiveness and mercy for the nation's transgressions. Following these prayers of repentance, he received an angelic visitation from Gabriel. The heavens opened to him even though he was living in the most brutal, heathen nation of his day.

2. Worship

You can create a portal of glory when you worship the Lord. I believe this happened at the dedication of Solomon's temple when the Lord filled the building with His glory presence.

I once heard a testimony about a gathering in South America, where over 60,000 believers met in a particular city to worship. As they worshiped, people in the surrounding region, who were not at the worship gathering, began to get saved. In addition, the fear of the Lord began to visit those in the area who were involved in corruption. A portal of glory had been opened through the power of corporate worship.

3. Tithes and Offerings

In Malachi, the Lord spoke strongly through the prophet, accusing His people of robbing Him by withholding tithes and offerings. He explained to them that their sin had placed them under a curse.

God then gave them a plan of action:

> *"Bring the whole tithe into the storehouse, so that there may be food in My house, and test Me now in this," says the LORD of hosts, "if I will not* ***open for you the windows of heaven*** *and pour out for you a blessing until it overflows. Then I will rebuke the devourer for you"* (Mal. 3:10,11, emphasis mine).

My husband and I have seen this promise work over and over again in our own lives. Giving tithes and offerings to the Lord has opened a portal of glory over our lives—it will for you, too.

4. Obedience

Deuteronomy 28:1,2 promises that as we obey the commandments of the Lord, we will be overtaken by blessings. One of those blessings (v. 12) is "the open heaven."

5. Prayer

In Matthew 6, Jesus taught us to pray for the Kingdom of God to come and for the Father's will to be done on the earth as it is in heaven. In other words, He was inviting us to pray for the opening of portals of glory through which heaven can come to earth.

A study of historical revivals of the Church reveals that prayer movements precede spiritual revival and harvest. In the Welsh Revival in 1904, fervent prayer and intercession opened a heavenly portal that influenced the entire nation of Wales and many other parts of the earth.

Fervent, unified prayer has also been the catalyst for the recent transformation of some communities around the world. God keeps His promises. He says in 2 Chronicles 7:13,14,

> *If I shut up the heavens… and My people who are called by My name humble themselves and pray and seek My face and turn from their wicked ways, then I will hear from heaven, will forgive their sin and will heal their land.*

Prayer is one key to opening a closed heaven. Combined with humility, repentance, and true seeking of the Lord, prayer will insure the healing of the land.

The disciples understood this promise. In Acts 1:14 they engage in continuous, united prayer. The outcome (found in chapter 2)—an open heaven. They were all filled with the Holy Spirit and over 3,000 were added to the Church in a single day. Now *that* is an open heaven!

Opening Heaven Over Your Life

Like the disciples, you can expect an open heaven over your life. Imagine how wonderful it will be to enjoy the Lord's abundant blessings in your life, in your church, in your city and in your nation. Portals of glory are opening up all over the world. Heaven is touching earth. Heaven wants to touch you!

Third Heaven Intercession

While engaging in a strategic prayer time with a number of renowned intercession leaders, an angel appeared in our midst. Only a couple of individuals actually saw the angelic visitor, while most of the others had a strong witness and a sense of its presence. We began to inquire of the Lord as to why the celestial creature had appeared to us. He made it clear that He was giving us invitation to rise up to a level of third heaven perspective in our intercession for the particular global project we were praying for. The angel had actually been sent to encourage us to rise up into this new level of corporate intercessory prayer perspective. We were being called to execute spiritual authority into the earth from a "third heaven position."

In an earlier chapter, we discovered that the Scriptures declare we are positioned in the heavenly places with Christ Jesus (see Eph. 1,2). Most of the time, we view life from an earthly perspective, rather than a heavenly one. In doing so, we are often overwhelmed by the pressing and oppressive circumstances that might be glaring at us.

Demonic warfare and oppression is usually launched from the second heaven. This is believed to be the place from which demonic hierarchy rules. Knowing this confirms it would be extremely helpful for us to be aware of our position in the third heaven as we fight the good fight of faith. It is better to be postured "above and not beneath." It is God Himself who is both truth and wisdom, and we happen to be His children as well as His Kingdom ambassadors. His truth, wisdom, power, and authority have been freely granted to us, and we have been given an open invitation to boldly access the throne of grace in our time of need (see 1 Cor. 1:30; John 14:6; Matt. 28:18–20).

In our attempt to receive revelation concerning the third heaven intercessory posture of the believer, it might be helpful for us to understand Christ's offices of Priest, Prophet, and King. Christ stands forever in these functions, and as believers, we are to release the authority of these offices into the earth.

Priests

Jesus is referred to in Scripture as our "High Priest." His priesthood is eternal and His position is in the throne room. Hebrews 8:1 declares,

> *Now the main point in what has been said is this: we have such a high priest, who has taken His seat at the right hand of the throne of the Majesty in the heavens.* [Chapters 2–9 in the book of Hebrews offers an in-depth study into the priesthood of Christ.]

The duties of the priest are intercessory. The Old Testament priests were to offer blood sacrifices for the sins of the people so that transgressions could be remitted, resulting in a restored relationship between God and His people. Christ, through His death on the cross, has now become the ultimate sacrifice, and His blood has been shed for all people and for all time. He forever stands "in the gap" for us.

> *Therefore He is able also to save forever those who draw near to God through Him, since He always lives to make intercession for them* (Heb 7:25).

As New Testament priests, like our Old Testament counterparts, our role is also intercessory. We do not, however, need to kill a sacrificial animal anymore, and neither do we need to perform ceremonial rituals for the remission of sins. We are simply required to appropriate by faith the divine blood that has already been shed. The New Testament church in its priestly role can stand in the gap for sinners, proclaiming the power of the redeeming sacrifice over their lives. This act of intercession is the greatest key for revival and harvest. This act of faith and obedience actually grants the Lord a landing strip and entry point to move powerfully in the lives of the wayward.

When we look from an earthly perspective at a person engaged in vile sin, we sometimes tend to lose heart and faith. The vileness of sin frequently appears to be more powerful than Christ's righteousness. Situations often seem like impossibilities in the light of the transformation that is needed. In the midst of a crisis, concerned Christians might cry out to God with intense passion, hoping and praying that their pleas will somehow, someway, reach His hearing. Oftentimes following such travail, they find themselves disappointed in the results. They continue to feel overwhelmed by the adverse circumstances and pressures that appear to be much more luminous than the hope they embrace. In this case, their "earthly" perspective influences their emotions and focus.

Intercession from a third heaven posture, however, draws us to a different point of view. The third heaven is the place of Christ's established rule and authority. *"All authority has been given to Me in heaven and on earth,"* Christ proclaimed clearly in Matthew 28:18. In the light of this Scripture, we can have absolute assurance that the power and authority found in Christ is well able to cleanse, purify, and redeem any sin and any measure of it. The vilest of sinner can be completely and fully delivered from the power of the sins that bind them through an intercessor that is willing to stand in the gap until the manifestation of divine truth is realized in the sinner's life.

This is very evident when we look from the perspective of truth and from the position of His ruling authority. Let us review some Scripture that we have studied in a previous chapter to reassure us of our position with Christ in the heavenly places:

> *That the God of our Lord Jesus Christ, the Father of glory, may give to you a spirit of wisdom and of revelation in the knowledge of Him. I pray that the eyes of your heart may be enlightened, so that you will know what is the hope of His calling, what are the riches of*

> *the glory of His inheritance in the saints, and what is the surpassing greatness of His power toward us who believe. These are in accordance with the working of the strength of His might which He brought about in Christ, when He raised Him from the dead and seated Him at His right hand in the heavenly places, far above all rule and authority and power and dominion, and every name that is named, not only in this age but also in the one to come. And He put all things in subjection under His feet, and gave Him as head over all things to the church, which is His body, the fullness of Him who fills all in all* (Eph. 1:17–23).

> *But God, being rich in mercy, because of His great love with which He loved us, even when we were dead in our transgressions, made us alive together with Christ (by grace you have been saved), and raised us up with Him, and seated us with Him in the heavenly places in Christ Jesus* (Eph. 2:4–6).

This Scripture is very clear that we are seated in the heavenly places *"in Christ."* If Christ is indeed *"priestly"* (or intercessory) and we are *"in Him,"* then we, as New Testament believers, can also walk in His priestly authority and function.

A friend of mine had received Christ, but her husband was not yet born again. He seemed to be somewhat indifferent to the gospel and after a while became intolerant of her spiritual passion and hunger. She was very discouraged and overwhelmed by the tension that was in their marriage. One day during her prayer time, the Lord drew her into a throne room perspective and assured her of His promise to save her household if she would stand in faith. She suddenly was filled with a release of faith. With confidence she could pray, "Let Your Kingdom come; let Your will be done in my husband's life on earth as it is settled today in heaven." She was filled with a supernatural strength to stand in the gap for her husband's salvation. Her faith waxed strong as she now had the "intercessory promise" and it came right from the throne room!

Prophets

Jesus is not only priestly in His function, but His role is also prophetic. Revelation 19:10 says, *"the testimony of Jesus is the spirit of prophecy."* Prophecy refers to communication that comes from the heart of God, and it often fulfills a futuristic role. In Revelation 4:1, we find the Lord giving John an invitation: *"Come up here, and I will show you what must take place after these things."* As John was called up into the throne room of God, he was promised prophetic insight.

During third heaven experiences, the Lord will often reveal His plans and purposes for the future, or give prophetic insight into a current situation. Prophetic insight will always aid in effective intercessory prayer. Anna the prophetess was in the temple praying day and night for over sixty years (see Luke 2). You will notice that she was both priestly (intercessory) and prophetic. The prophetic will reveal to us the will of God and then we will know how to pray and release the will of the Lord into the earth. The Lord is looking for those who will birth His purposes.

Prophetic revelation can be received in a number of different ways. Sometimes when I am accessing the third heaven in worship, I will receive a vision or an impression, while other times the Word of the Lord comes through a still small voice or a quiet thought. The prophetic involves three parts that require insight: revelation, interpretation, and application.

Your third heaven experiences will at times contain prophetic symbolism that lacks clear understanding. Prayer to receive interpretation is, of course, vital in a case like this. After you have understanding what the word or vision means, it is also important to receive the insight on how to apply it.

When I was first beginning to access the third heaven realm by faith, I had a prophetic experience. As I was "descending" from the throne room, I saw a vision of snow-capped mountains, trees, and eagles' nests with eagles gathering together. The understanding came that the snow-capped mountains represented a region in the Pacific Northwest and the eagles represented a company of prophets that would gather. The very next day, a friend was having a third heaven experience and saw almost the identical vision without knowing what I had seen the day before. Within six months of these experiences, my friend was involved in organizing, leading, and hosting a significant gathering of prophets. I helped her with the project, and during the months following the vision, we engaged in prayer for the Lord's purposes in the prophetic gathering to be accomplished. On the day the prophets arrived for the meeting, there was a fresh snowfall on the mountains that surrounded our city. A company of prophets had gathered in the region of snow-capped mountains. What we had seen in our third heaven prophetic experience had now literally been "downloaded" into the earthly realm.

Through our placement in the throne room of God, we can stand in the counsel of the Lord. In Jeremiah 23:22, the Lord communicates concerning the prophets,

> *"But if they had stood in My council, Then they would have announced My words to My people, And would have turned them back from their evil way And from the evil of their deeds."*

As believers we can stand in the Lord's presence and receive His prophetic counsel. This counsel will give us insight and wisdom and will enable us to be effective in prayer and in leading people to righteousness.

Kings

The Lord is referred to in Scripture as the "King of Kings" (see Rev. 19:16). In Psalm 24, we see the Lord called "the King of glory." Kingly anointing is in reference to Christ's rule and authority and is necessary for effective intercession. We are called to be people who operate in His kingly anointing in the earth and who will "settle issues," bringing forth divine order. As we access the third heaven, we will be able to receive His Word, His ability to stand in the gap, and also the mandate to release His authority and power into the earth.

The Lord is raising up His kingdom ambassadors who will bring His word of counsel to the kings of the earth. Recently we have received many reports and testimonies concerning government leaders who are asking the Church not only for prayer, but also for counsel and insight on civic and national affairs. These invitations for godly wisdom are going to increase in the days to come as more and more believers stand in the third heaven counsel chambers of the Lord. Many politicians, economists, scientists, educators, and financiers are crying out for answers and insights that they do not have at this time. God is preparing sanctified vessels to step into this ambassadorial role.

Believers who know the heart, will, and counsel of God will be able to grant understanding and confrontation during these strategic times. As Joseph and Daniel were raised up in perilous times as "kings" before the people, so also shall the Church today. As Moses stood before Pharaoh and demonstrated God's power and authority, so also shall those who are prepared to be His standard-bearers in this hour. As Elijah confronted the false prophets with a demonstration of God's might, so also shall the Lord's body confront the corruption in our day.

The Lord is calling those who are willing to stand in His presence, in His glory and in His counsel. He is calling for those who will stand in the gap as prophets, priests, and kings. We are all being called up higher into a third heaven perspective. Lord, help us respond. Help us stand.

Heavenly Provision

Your heavenly Father knows what you are in need of. He has opened the heavens so that you will have more than enough to enjoy a life of abundance. True Bible prosperity offers the child of God enough resources and provisions to honor and bless the Lord, to have all personal needs met, and have enough left over to help meet the needs of others. Believers are called to this abundance. Great measures of Kingdom blessing await every child of God.

In The Beginning

Genesis 1:26–30 reads,

Then God said, "Let Us make man in Our image, according to Our likeness; and let them rule over the fish of the sea and over the birds of the sky and over the cattle and over all the earth, and over every creeping thing that creeps on the earth." God

> *created man in His own image, in the image of God He created him; male and female He created them. God blessed them; and God said to them, "Be fruitful and multiply, and fill the earth, and subdue it; and rule over the fish of the sea and over the birds of the sky and over every living thing that moves on the earth." Then God said, "Behold, I have given you every plant yielding seed that is on the surface of all the earth, and every tree which has fruit yielding seed; it shall be food for you; and to every beast of the earth and to every bird of the sky and to every thing that moves on the earth which has life, I have given every green plant for food"; and it was so.*

In the beginning, Adam and Eve had more than enough. They had been created in the image of God, were in perfect fellowship with Him, and had been granted dominion over every living thing that moved upon the earth. Their provision was sure and they had been blessed by God to *"be fruitful and multiply"* (Gen. 1:28). Fruitfulness spoke of the success that would follow everything that man put his hand to. Mankind was to be fruitful and successful. He was given the ability to experience multiplication of blessing in his life and to fill the earth with it.

Prior to the fall, man did not know what "toil" was. His stewardship of the earth was sheer joy for him as he co-labored with God through intimate friendship with Him. He didn't need to labor against any resistance in order to secure a living for himself. He was not acquainted with fear or pressure. He was at peace, rest, and was fully satisfied. All was blessed by God, and Adam and Eve lived under that canopy of blessing.

The Fall and the Curse

In Genesis 3 we find that man transgressed the boundaries of the Lord and as a result came under a curse. God's boundaries are established to allow us to experience freedom, liberty, and goodness within safe perimeters. He is like a shepherd who prepares a rich green pasture for his sheep. The pasture has a pure water source, as well as a luxurious field to graze in. To protect from elements and predators that might harm the sheep, the shepherd erects a fence or a boundary. The boundary serves as a means to keep the sheep within the blessings so they can fully enjoy the richness of the pasture without harm. Boundaries are healthy and it is wise to embrace them.

We find many Christians who transgress the boundaries set in the principles of the Word of God and, of course, the transgressions almost always produce painful consequences. Adam and Eve certainly suffered the consequences of transgressing boundaries and unfortunately their choices affected all mankind for all the ages to come.

Genesis 3:17–19 describes a curse that came on the ground and upon Adam's ability to bring forth fruit from the earth:

> *Then to Adam He said, "Because you have listened to the voice of your wife, and have eaten*

> *from the tree about which I commanded you, saying, 'You shall not eat from it'; Cursed is the ground because of you; In toil you will eat of it All the days of your life. Both thorns and thistles it shall grow for you; And you will eat the plants of the field; By the sweat of your face You will eat bread, Till you return to the ground, Because from it you were taken; For you are dust, And to dust you shall return."*

Transgression comes at a huge price, and as we can see in this passage, Adam's consequences included:

1. Cursed ground.
2. Eating of the ground in sorrow all the days of his life.
3. Thorns and thistles coming forth from the ground.
4. Making a living through sweat and toil.
5. Physical death.

This is quite a paradigm shift from the original *"be fruitful and multiply."* As well as other severe ramifications of the fall, these consequences have visited all mankind from the point of Adam's "fatal error."

Restored in Christ

Ever since the fall, we have experienced resistance to a life of ease and fruitfulness. We are often plagued with fears as to how we will manage to make ends meet. We strive and contend for position in order to get ahead financially in a competitive world. Unfortunately, many of these mindsets are also found within the church. Numerous believers are afraid of not having enough provisions or resources to maintain a comfortable life, let alone an abundant one. These mindsets are not Christ-like.

In Christ, we have been delivered from sin and its consequences:

> *For the law of the Spirit of life in Christ Jesus has set you free from the law of sin and of death* (Rom. 8:2).

In Christ, every spiritual blessing in the heavenly places has been granted to us:

> *Blessed be the God and Father of our Lord Jesus Christ, who has blessed us with every spiritual blessing in the heavenly places in Christ* (Eph. 1:3).

In Christ, we have been promised that everything we have need of to live a godly and righteous life has been granted, giving us the privilege of partaking of His divine nature and escaping the corruption that is in the world system.

> *Grace and peace be multiplied to you in the knowledge of God and of Jesus our Lord; seeing that His divine power has granted to us everything pertaining to life and godliness, through the true knowledge of Him who called us by His own glory and excellence. For by these He has granted to us His precious and magnificent promises, so that by them you may become partakers of the divine nature, having escaped the corruption that is in the world by lust* (2 Pet. 1:2–4).

In Christ, we have assurance of an abundant life:

> *"The thief comes only to steal and kill and destroy; I came that they may have life, and have it abundantly"* (John 10:10).

In Christ, we have been made rich through His choice to take our poverty to the cross:

> *For you know the grace of our Lord Jesus Christ, that though He was rich, yet for your sake He became poor, so that you through His poverty might become rich* (2 Cor. 8:9).

It is definitely God's desire for His people to prosper. Third John 2 says, *"Beloved, I pray that in all respects you may prosper and be in good health, just as your soul prospers."* This prosperity is not only for individuals, but there is an inversion of wealth that is coming to the Church in general so that the Body of Christ will have resources to care for the poor and the needy of the nations (note the prophetic word, "Great Wealth, Great Warning" at the end of this chapter). The Lord said to the children of Israel in Deuteronomy 8:18,

> *"But you shall remember the LORD your God, for it is He who is giving you power to make wealth, that He may confirm His covenant which He swore to your fathers, as it is this day."*

Like Abraham, we are created to be blessed and to be a blessing. The nations of the earth will be blessed through God's covenant people (see Gen. 12:2,3). All our needs are met *"according to His riches in glory in Christ Jesus"* (Phil. 4:19).

Personal Testimony

Prior to being launched into a full-time preaching ministry, my husband Ron and I served the Lord in the secular arena. I served as a nurse in a local hospital and Ron in the transport industry. Both of our employment situations provided a comfortable lifestyle for our family. We loved our work, and following our conversion, we had numerous opportunities to share God's love and power with those we came in contact with at our respective places of employment.

In 1980, the Lord called us to leave our ministry in the secular field in order to pursue Bible training that would prepare us for service in evangelism and missions. The decision to respond to this call included the downsizing of all we owned. We gave away many of our possessions and took a giant step of faith. We had enough finances available to travel with our two children to the training center in Hawaii and to care for all our material needs for about a year. We learned so much during that time and felt a strong leading of the Lord to continue living with a mission's focus.

On our return home to Canada, we were invited to serve in our church in a local evangelism leadership role. We enjoyed the assignment and were used to equip and mobilize believers into prayer and evangelism. This was a volunteer position. A financial recession had hit at this particular time and there was very little employment available. Despite our diligent, daily efforts to secure employment, our endeavors continuously fell short of our expectation.

During prayer one day, the Lord revealed that He was inviting us to begin a journey of living by supernatural provision. He was calling us to live by faith, to believe Him to literally supply our daily bread. He also made it clear that during this time we were not allowed to share our needs with anyone and neither were we to receive funds from government agencies. (Some people are released to receive government help in crisis and that is completely acceptable; but in this particular situation, we were instructed not to.) At first the invitation seemed to promise exciting adventures that would produce glorious testimonies, but it didn't take long to feel the pressure of a demonic assignment that targeted us in painstaking ways for the next five years. Sometimes when the enemy sees the potential of God's grace being released through an individual, he will assault with an intentional, strategic assignment to completely destroy the individual and their calling (see John 10:10).

Early in the season of attack, we determined to stand on the Word and the promises of God concerning provision. We searched the Scriptures from Genesis through Revelation and found consistent and sure promises of providence for the Lord's covenant children. We began to confess the Word of God every day and by faith secured the precious promises. We prayed, fasted, and walked in faithful obedience to the Lord in regards to His instructions concerning resources, and yet, it seemed that our situation became increasingly under attack. To be absolutely honest, the assault was brutal. We were being oppressed by poverty and lack, and yet all the promises in the Word indicated freedom and liberty in the area of resources. Of course we processed many things over the years, but we consistently renewed our commitment to stand on the Word of God no matter what. We had no Plan B. "If God said it, He will make it good," we often reminded ourselves. "He is not a liar, but is the God of all truth" (John 14:6).

Through God's grace, we were enabled to keep the faith. After five years, the breakthrough came in a day. The Lord gave us a "suddenly." I actually felt the spiritual warfare break at a specific moment during a prayer time. We had tenaciously and aggressively held on to the promises and now the victory was won. Following that breakthrough moment, it was as if *"the heavens were opened"* (Matt. 3:16). Everything changed after that time and provision was released on every side.

It was following the securing of that victory that the Lord called us to labor in Tijuana, Mexico, a city that was plagued with poverty. By faith, we ventured out with a team of enthusiastic young people, determined to preach good news to the poor. In the natural, we had no visible means of support, but we had faith in the Lord's promises and began to pray for everything we needed to fulfill this great commission. As a result, the Lord's provision poured in and we were enabled to feed and clothe the poor everyday and to help build orphanages, medical centers, churches, and homes for the poor. We preached the gospel daily and witnessed the salvation of many souls. We distributed Bibles and gospel materials, established a evangelism training center, and were never touched by lack. When you secure a victory in the heavenlies, the victory stays with you and becomes your position of operative authority. All the grueling battles over the five years had prepared us to secure provision for Kingdom advancement and we have been blessed ever since.

The heaven is full of provisions that can be secured by believers through faith. At times, one might find themselves engaged in a second heaven level of warfare prior to the manifestation of the provisional miracle in the earthly realm. At these times, perseverance becomes vital in order to establish operative authority for the long term.

Kingdom resources await all of God's children. We are promised what we need to enjoy a life that is overflowing with blessings and to fulfill every assignment that the Lord puts in our hearts. The following are some helpful principles to help you secure heavenly provision:

1. Tithes and offerings will open the heavens for you (read Mal. 3).
2. You will reap what you sow. Sow in faith and reap in faith (Gen. 8:22; 2 Cor. 9:6–12).
3. Access the blessings in the heavenly places by faith (review the chapter entitled "Faith 'The Connector to Heavenly Glory'").
4. Confess the promises in the Word of God regarding provision. (A Word confession for the release of resource and provision is available to you at the end of this chapter.)
5. Ask the Lord to grant you wisdom. In wisdom are riches, honor, and long life (Prov. 8:18–21). Wisdom will teach you how to steward and manage resources and provisions.

6. Invite the Lord to dispatch angels from the resource department in heaven (review the chapter entitled "Honkin' Big Angels and Chariots Rides").
7. Walk in obedience. In Deuteronomy 28:1–13, the Scriptures teach that when you obey the Lord and His commandments, glorious blessings will *"come upon you and overtake you"* (v. 2).

A WORD CONFESSION FOR THE RELEASE OF RESOURCES AND PROVISIONS

I seek first the Kingdom of God, and His righteousness; and all the things I need shall be added unto me. I acknowledge that all of my needs are met according to my God's riches in glory by Christ Jesus. I do not fear for it is my Father's good pleasure to give me the Kingdom. Grace and peace are multiplied unto me through the knowledge of God and of Jesus my Lord. His divine power has given me all things that pertain unto life and godliness, through the knowledge of Him that has called me to glory and virtue. Blessed be the God and Father of my Lord Jesus Christ, who has blessed me with every spiritual blessing in the heavenly places in Christ. The Lord is a sun and a shield to me and will give me grace and glory. No good thing will He withhold from me as I walk uprightly (Matt. 6:33; Phil. 4:19; Luke 12:32; 2 Pet. 1:2,3; Eph. 1:3; Ps. 84:11).

I choose to sow bountifully, therefore I will reap bountifully. I give to the Lord, to His people, and to the needy as I purpose in my heart to give. I do not give grudgingly or out of compulsion, for my God loves a cheerful giver. God makes all grace abound towards me, that I always have enough for all things so that I may abound unto every good work. The Lord supplies seed for me to sow and bread for my food. He also supplies and multiplies my seed for sowing and increases the fruits of my righteousness. I am enriched in everything unto great abundance, which brings much thanksgiving to God (2 Cor. 9:6–11).

I bring all my tithes into the Lord's storehouse, so that there is meat in His house. As a result He opens up the windows of heaven and pours out a blessing for me so that there is not room enough to contain it. He rebukes the devourer for my sake, so that he does not destroy the fruits of my ground and neither does my vine cast its grapes before the time. All the nations shall call me blessed for I shall have a delightful life. I am blessed because I consider the poor. Because I give freely to the poor I will never want. My righteousness endures forever (Ps. 41:1; Ps. 112:1a,9; Prov. 28:27; Mal. 3:8–12).

I remember the Lord my God, for it is He who gives me the power to make wealth, that He may confirm His covenant. Because Jesus Christ, my Savior, diligently listened to the voice of God and obeyed all the commandments, the Lord will set me high above all the nations of the earth and all the blessings in the Kingdom shall come upon me and overtake me. Christ became poor so that through His poverty I might become rich. Jesus came so that I would have life in its abundance (Deut. 8:18; 28:1,22; 2 Cor. 8:9; John 10:10).

GREAT WEALTH—GREAT WARNING*

A Prophetic Word through Pat Coking, June 2001

GREAT WEALTH

Open heavens in the area of material provision are going to be experienced by many Kingdom believers who have prepared their hearts in the presence of the Lord. The Lord's eyes are moving to and fro to search out those whose hearts are completely His. He will show Himself strong on their behalf.

Divine resources and provisions will be released in copious measures to many who will follow the leading of the Spirit in areas of helping the poor, the outcasts, the destitute, and the widows and orphans.

Particular individuals anointed by God will carry fresh apostolic vision and burdens in the area of equipping, business, entrepreneurship, outreach and missions. They will lead the Body with a true gospel model. They will preach to the poor, heal the sick, and work the miraculous in order to reach the needs of the broken and bring the gospel to the nations. The Lord will be honoring their love and faith by releasing increased empowerment, favor, and resource.

Many Christians will come into unexpected financial blessing and increase within this next season. The Lord will test their hearts and will be watching for those who are trustworthy stewards of Kingdom provision. Those who are found to carry a single Kingdom focus will be

*"*Great Wealth, Great Warning" was a prophetic word that came through Pat Coking on June 29, 2001. It has been slightly edited by Pat in order to clarify/enhance what the Lord had originally revealed. The prophetic content of the original word and vision as she received it has not been altered.*

rewarded with a second wave of blessing that will far exceed the first.

Churches and Christian organizations that are willing to seek the Lord afresh for His heart for the lost in this season, will come into a new level of fulfillment in the area of intimacy with the Lord, which will be followed by increased resources. Deep pruning will take place during these seeking periods, which will prepare the church and individuals for greater fruitfulness and supernatural providence. Many leaders will find themselves laying down their current ministries and church structures in order to wait on the Lord. They will be very aware of the fact that, *"Unless the LORD builds the house, They labor in vain who build it"* (Ps. 127:1).

The apostolic ministry in the Body of Christ is going to move along a path of maturation and testing. The maturing of the apostolic anointing in the Body will produce new levels of unity and oneness in the corporate Body on a global level. Persecutions, as well as visitations of the Lord's presence in power, will strengthen this process and produce a true apostolic movement exhibiting Kingdom humility, power, and purity. Great grace, power, and provision will earmark the maturing of the apostolic foundations in the Church.

> *And with great power the apostles were giving testimony to the resurrection of the Lord Jesus, and abundant grace was upon them all. For there was not a needy person among them, for all who were owners of land or houses would sell them and bring the proceeds of the sales and lay them at the apostles' feet, and they would be distributed to each as any had need* (Acts 4:33–35).

False apostles will also surface during this time. These will be individuals who lust after power and resource and who carry personal agendas. They will witness the abundance of favor on the true apostolic river and will desire to reap the rewards without paying the price. The evidence of a crucified life that will manifest authentic Kingdom resurrection power will earmark the true apostolic gift.

Great Warning

The *"love of money"* is defined in the Scriptures as being *"the root of all evil"* (see 1 Tim. 6:10, KJV). The love of money is also the force that strengthens the "Babylonian system," through which all the world's buying and selling is based (see Rev. 18).

In this coming season of provisional outpouring, impure motives will surface in many people. Love for the world, for money, and for selfish gain will result in many choosing the path of Babylon rather than the Kingdom. The end result of choosing the Babylonian journey is destruction, great loss, and sorrow, whereas *"It is the blessing of the LORD that makes rich, And He adds no sorrow to it"* (Prov. 10:22).

It is imperative that believers watch over their hearts with all diligence for from the heart spring the issues of life. Deception and unclean motives in the area of finance and provision will cause individuals to perish and their silver with them (see Acts 8:18–23; also: the examples of Judas in Matt. 26:14–16; 27:3–5, and Ananias and Sapphira in Acts 5:1–11). This is a severe warning. *"Every man's way is right in his own eyes, But the LORD weighs the hearts"* (Prov. 21:2).

The Lord *will* be weighing the motives of His people and many will be found wanting in the balance.

A Specific Warning to Pastors, Leaders, and Itinerant Ministers

The Lord is looking to abundantly bless those whose hearts are completely His with new levels of anointing, empowerment, gifting, favor, creativity, strategy in business, and resources. Many leaders and Kingdom spokesmen will experience these new levels of blessing and will be granted fresh apostolic strategies from the Lord. The Lord will be initiating new areas of outreach and ministry in the market place, in the streets, and in the church. This will result in an increased harvest of souls and Kingdom advancement.

The enemy is lurking, however, and will attempt to move some leaders out of faith, focus, and trust, and into strategies that are not born of the Spirit. Three visions were given regarding this on June 29, 2001:

1. The Glittering Snake: In a vision, a snake was seen that was fully studded with precious gems. It was glittering and shimmering and could barely be seen for what it truly was due to the splendor of its appearance. The glittering effect was influencing and enticing leaders. When the leaders in the vision were captured by delight in the extravagance of the gems, they moved towards the serpent to touch and to handle the gems. As they did, the snake began to wrap itself around the body of the individual. The victim (representing leaders) did not actually physically die in the vision but, in fact, wore the gem-clad snake as a garment. The others were not really aware of the serpent as it was well hidden in the massive extravagance of the jewels and glitter. They enjoyed being arrayed in the glitter but did not realize the source.

Interpretation: This vision sounds a warning to the Body (especially leaders), that demon powers will attempt to appeal to the lusts of man's flesh and soulish desires in this next season. This appeal will specifically target the heart in areas of personal love for money and provision. If given into, the temptation will wrap leaders in demonic, worldly bondage and thus cause them to misrepresent Christ and His Kingdom. Worldly and demonic glitter will then manifest, rather than the nature of Christ. *"There is a way which seems right to a man, But its end is the way of death"* (Prov. 14:12).

2. The Hounds: Demonic hound dogs were seen in a vision, sniffing out the "ground of blessing." When they came to a place where they could smell a pool of blessing beneath the earth, they began to furiously dig through the soil. When they hit the level where the blessings were situated (seen in the vision as golden bones), they laid hold of them with a firm grip in their teeth and jaws and ran away with their treasure.

Interpretation: The hounds represented demonic spirits who were looking to take for themselves that which they did not prepare or plant. The vision gave a sense of warning to leaders: to be watchful for the temptation to take from another's gifting or resource pool. The area of motives in ministry relationships needs to be carefully watched over.

3. The Leeches: Black leeches were seen sucking onto a healthy body.

Interpretation: The black leeches represented individuals with impure motives who wanted to take (not just receive but TAKE) from gifted members of the Body to feed themselves. This could indicate areas of anointing, favor, reputation, and resource.

The Place of Protection

Not even one individual needs to fall into the prementioned traps and temptations. It is the Father's desire to freely give His children all things, and in this coming season to bring about a flow of blessing to and through His people such as history has never known. Every child of God is a candidate to receive the manifestation of this outpouring. The Father wants to confirm His covenant and to bless His people in order to make them a blessing (see Gen. 12:1–3 and Deut. 8:18).

The following are some ways that you can prepare to stand in the midst of the coming outpouring of His kindness:

1. Spend time in His Presence; seek His face.
2. Submit yourself completely to the Lord and His Word.
3. Remain in love and faith.
4. Clothe yourself in humility.
5. Resist temptation, especially in the areas of the love of money, power, and reputation.

Some Scriptures for Meditation:

- Haggai 1,2
- Matthew 6:19–34
- James 4:3–10
- Deuteronomy 8

Nuts, Flakes, and Weirdos

Have you ever attended prayer meetings, church services, or prophetic groups where someone who appears to be very "spiritual" seems to create a corporate disruption, leaving people feeling very disturbed? There is a distinct possibility that your meeting was disturbed by a "nut-flake-or-weirdo," from here on referred to as an "NFW." However, not all unusual occurrences in meetings are created by NFWs—they could be a result of a legitimate move of God. When the Holy Spirit moves in power, He often causes some very strange and unique manifestations which may leave **some** people feeling uncomfortable. God also sometimes causes His people to do strange things for good reasons.

When I think of John the Baptist, I wonder how I would have handled the guy, had I lived at that time. *My, my! Eating locusts? Yelling out in the wilderness?*

What would most of us have done with Isaiah if, walking down the street on our way to the market one day, we found this so-called "prophet" strutting around naked and barefoot? (See Isa. 20:2,3.) Our reaction might be a little sceptical: "Sure, Isaiah—like we *really* believe the Lord told you to streak for three years."

And then there's Ezekiel, who made little barley cakes mixed with dung (see Ezek. 4:12–15). Imagine his explanation: "Yeppers, it's the new food for prophets—and God gave me the recipe!"

So, what do we do with all this? How do we discern the difference between an NFW and the real thing? What is the difference between religious delusion and true spiritual encounter?

Any time the Lord does something new in His Body, you will discover a pure stream of God's Spirit and alongside of it you will find the "Ex-streams." One of those Ex-streams contains fleshly defilement and fanaticism. In another Ex-stream, you will find the legalists who persecute and oppose the true stream. This pattern of pure stream and Ex-streams is consistent throughout historical revivals and moves of the Spirit.

As we embrace spiritual experience, it is important to discern the true from the false. Leaders need to learn to pastor, mentor and teach their people about the new things God is doing. This process can be messy, uncomfortable, and challenging. Sometimes it might seem easier to just "can" the whole thing and shut down the moving of the Spirit.

However, we mustn't "throw the baby out with the bathwater." Think of the scenario of teaching children to eat food on their own. The first time you put the spoon into their little hands, food seems to go everywhere but in their mouth. They get gravy in their hair, mushed up peas on their t-shirts, and chocolate pudding smeared all over their faces, hands, and legs.

They're happy though—their grins are as big as their faces. It takes a lot of extra work to wash their faces and hands, shampoo their hair, launder the t-shirts, and clean up the high chairs, the floors, and any place else where the "food experience" splattered. We could say, "Forget this! I will feed you from now on! You make too much of a mess! The new family rule is that only Mom or Dad can feed the kids!" Oh, sure! That might work for a while, but it will look pretty pathetic when you are still hand-feeding your twenty-year-old.

Progress, maturity, and growth can often be messy. So, too, is the maturing process of something new in the Body of Christ. Great discernment, patience, and wisdom are required. In the area of spiritual experiences, heavenly encounters, and angelic visitations there is potential for error—consequently, good guidelines and scriptural perimeters are necessary. Driving an automobile on a busy street is also potentially dangerous, but it doesn't mean we should never learn to drive. We simply need to learn the rules of the road, abide by the perimeters set by the law, and proceed with care.

Examining the Fruit

Jesus said that we would know a tree by its fruit. He taught that a good tree would not bear bad fruit and a bad tree would not bear good fruit (see Matt. 7:17–19). I have personally seen many things in the Body of Christ over the last number of years that have made my hair stand on end. These situations need to be examined and evaluated according to Scripture and fruit that is evident in a person's life.

What Is Going on in Your Heart?

One test I have found helpful is to ask the person who is being "influenced" what is going on in his or her heart. God always looks at the heart, while man looks at the outward appearance. This is always a good place to start. Most of the time, an individual will be able to share with you what the Lord is doing in or through them at the moment. It is good to listen and then to evaluate according to the plumbline of the Word of God. God is not the author of confusion and therefore the response should bring clarity.

Corporate Influence

Another test is to check out the "corporate influence." Is the overall well-being of the meeting disturbed? We have been in sessions where there were some very unusual things transpiring and yet there was a corporate peace, flow, and witness. At other times, however, there was unrest in the corporate group (or in individuals) accompanied by a sense of isolated or general disturbance. NFWs are often "out of the flow" of the corporate anointing. This is a sign that something might be "off" and needs further evaluation and investigation.

Sometimes, if a situation has been in question, we will organize a meeting with the person who is manifesting and also with some of those who have been disturbed by it. Many times, through honest dialogue, we are able to evaluate and assess the situation better. Good listening skills are important.

It is vital that believers learn to receive confrontation without absorbing rejection. Confrontation, of course, needs to be gentle (although sometimes firm), for wisdom from above is easily entreated (see Jas. 3:17).

I remember a particular incident that took place in a prayer group. One of the intercessors was engaging in loud, aggressive, "birthing and travailing" intercession in a meeting where the general flow of the session was not in that vein. Her intercession was extremely disturbing to the rest of the team. When she was invited to join the group in their direction, she explained that she couldn't because the Holy Spirit was leading her in a different way and that she had to complete her intercession. The rest of the prayer team was offended and did not know what to do. The "wailer and travailer" was also offended because she believed she was being unduly restrained from obeying the Holy Spirit.

We brought every member together and heard the heart of each individual involved. They explained how they were feeling at the time and what they sensed the Spirit was saying to them. It helped hearing each other's hearts. Following a time of sharing and prayer they invited the Lord to show them wisdom on how to keep the corporate unity and flow and yet facilitate the wailing and travailing prayer.

It was agreed that if the general flow of the meeting (which was to be determined by the prayer group leader) was not bearing witness to engaging in the birthing prayer, then the wailer and travailer would go into another room to complete her intercession. This would facilitate peace in the general prayer meeting allowing the members to carry on with an agreed-upon corporate flow. At the same time it gave honor and respect to what the wailer and travailer was carrying in her heart. She was in agreement with this.

There was humility and teachability in the hearts of all these individuals. These attributes do not usually accompany NFWs. However, in a case like this, you will want to keep a watch on the situation. If subsequent occurrences create discord or confusion, you might need to do some further investigation. You could possibly have someone in your group who needs some help, mentoring, or healing... or you might have an NFW that is in need of adjustment, discipline, and a whole lot of love!

Drawing Attention to Self

If individuals within groups perform acts which draw attention to themselves, there is room to be concerned. The focus in any spiritual experience should be Jesus—therefore, anything or anyone posing a distraction from that focus is a possible sign that an NFW is in your midst.

Often there is a sense of the individual in question moving independently from the rest of the group. For instance, sometimes in prayer meetings we find the leader giving direction to the group while an individual will be off in a corner engaged in something totally different. This person, when asked to join in with the others, usually *refuses* to join in and claims a belief that the Spirit is leading him or her "differently." This sense of separation, lack of submission, distraction, and independence from the rest of the prayer team often identifies an NFW.

Spiritual Antennas Are Agitated

We have found through experience that most NFWs create a reaction in sensitive prophetic intercessors and others in the Body. I remember a situation a few years ago where almost an entire church congregation was negatively stirred in their discernment concerning someone who desired to make this particular house of worship their church family. The spiritual antennas of the leadership team, intercessors, and church family were agitated. This is a sign that something is definitely "off." Jesus said that His sheep would hear His voice and they would **not** follow the voice of a stranger. He further said that His sheep would actually *flee* from a stranger (see John 10:4,5). The gift of the discerning of spirits is in believers and will be stirred when things are "not quite right." If many feel uncomfortable, beware! It is important to heed those checks in the spirit. They are God's warning signals.

When dealing with NFWs, we have at times found strong disagreement and resistance in their hearts towards what leaders are discerning. They will plead their case with Scripture and explanations that seem to make some sense. If, as a leader, you still have an uneasy feeling, a check in your spirit, or a subtle caution within after listening with openness to someone's heart, do *not* lay down your discernment! Stand in confidence. At times when my discernment has been challenged by an NFW, I have just had to explain, "I might be wrong, but at this time I am not comfortable and so I will stand in my discernment for now."

Favor with God and Man

A believer operating in true anointing should be growing in favor with the general Body of believers. Jesus grew in *"favor with God **and men**"* (see Luke 2:52, emphasis added). We have often heard an NFW claim to have a very intimate relationship with the Lord (even deeper than the average believer). While this person describes many spiritual experiences, there doesn't seem to be a general or growing favor with the Body of Christ. Often this is explained away by an NFW as the Body being religious and not understanding "true anointing."

Generally speaking, we find that if a person's horizontal relationships are not bearing fruit, there is more than likely something not quite right with their vertical relationship with God.

Jesus is a great example to us in the way that he related with people in the earth. His vertical relationship with His heavenly Father could not have been any closer and you will not find another more "spiritual" than Jesus Himself—yet, He related very well with those around Him. He grew in *"favor with God* and men"

Jesus was favored in the temple and the synagogues. We know that some in the "religious community" persecuted Him, but for the most part, He was favored in the House of the Lord. He preached in the synagogues and was called "Teacher" and "Rabbi." Sinners also favored Jesus. The multitudes, both sinner and saint, followed Him.

Jesus was also very practical and "down to earth," even though He was "heavenly." Sometimes we have found that NFWs have a difficult time relating to the practical dimension of life. It seems as though their head is in the clouds and there is not a clear connection to the natural realm in the earth. Jesus was so "normal" that some were very amazed at His reputation of being the Son of God, for they said, *"Is not this the carpenter's son?"* (Matt. 13:55). Jesus was incarnated into the human race and related well to the earthly realm. If we are truly heavenly-minded, we bear fruit in the natural dimension of life. If we are not being any earthly good, perhaps we should question our biblical foundations and spiritual experiences.

Offense and Bitterness

We have further discovered that NFWs frequently have a root of offense towards religious authority figures or leaders in the Body of Christ.

Offense is extremely dangerous. The moment we sow a seed of critical judgment and offense, we have actually drawn in to ourselves the very thing that we have judged and been offended by. I have seen this repeatedly and consistently. Many NFWs have roots of offense and bitter judgments in their lives that have stemmed out of some wounding from the past. Often they have trust issues that need to be healed.

A reservoir of water might be completely pure—however, the water that comes out of the tap will be defiled if there is rust in the pipe through which the water travels from the original source. This is how it works in the realm of the spirit as well. A believer has a pure pool of living water within, but if offense, bitterness, unhealed hurts, and judgments is in the soul, the gifts and blessings of the Lord will not be released in purity. The "rust" defiles the water.

Folks can get sick by drinking bad water. We have seen negative effects in those who have allied themselves with NFWs. Some pastors have testified that they have experienced NFWs sowing discord and dissension into their entire church family.

True spiritual believers walk in a heart of unity with the rest of the Body and demonstrate a submissive spirit especially to those in authority. They do not walk in or breed an independent attitude.

There are times when we might feel a strong conviction regarding something that differs from the teachings of our spiritual leaders or others in the Body. It is healthy to discuss these differences with a heart of honesty and truth and yet with utmost humility, respect, and honor. We must always remain teachable.

When we enter into spiritual experience, it is important that we are willing to be challenged by those who do not understand. Confrontation and challenge is healthy—it perfects and refines that which we believe. If our experience is truly from God, it will stand the test of the Word and the nature and character of God. This is part of being teachable and growing and maturing. NFWs often do not like to be challenged. Instead of being open, they become defensive during times of confrontation.

It is imperative that every believer has a strong circle of accountability around his or her life. Recently we dealt with an individual who had received specific direction from the Lord, through spiritual vision and revelatory experience, for her future. A number of mature Christians and leaders around her had very strong concerns and communicated that they felt she was in deception. She stood against their counsel and claimed that they didn't understand her call. She believed her call was on a higher level than what they understood. This is dangerous and life-threatening thinking!

Deception, Pride, and Leviathan

A love for truth will help keep you from deception. There are times, as Christians, when we may be touched by deception—but we can trust the Lord to deliver us if we have a love for truth. Deception is going to increase in the last days and it is important that we understand the dangers (see 2 Thess. 2:9,10; 1 Tim. 4:1,2,16; 2 Tim. 3:1–5,13; Matt. 24:4,5,11). Usually you will find some level of error in an NFW's doctrinal or theological interpretations.

When I was on a mission field, a number of years ago, I worked with some leaders who were deceived by legalism. They believed that, in order to please the Lord and to have relationship with Him, you had to really work at perfecting your life. They often pointed out things in my life that they believed were offensive to the Lord and demanded that I "bring things into line." These leaders were very zealous and genuinely loved the Lord, but they were deceived. At that point in my life, I did not know how to rightly divide the Word in that area and so I bought into the lie. I worked, struggled, and wrestled in order to bring my flesh into subjection, only to find that I couldn't perfect it. The pressure of all this self-effort left me desolate. I had been deceived.

On my return home, my church leaders pointed out to me the error I had entered into, and they helped me walk out of it. I was hungry for truth. When they spoke the truth to me, I recognized it. I had many questions as I journeyed through the healing process but the Lord honored my love for truth. Truth is a Person—Truth is Jesus. The Word is also truth. In John 17:17, the Scripture says, *"Sanctify them in the truth; Your word is truth."* That taste of deception immunized me from that point on. I can now "smell" a legalistic spirit from "a mile away." All things work together for good. Peter was deceived when he denied Christ—yet, when he came through, he became a valuable apostolic servant in the Kingdom of God. Jesus prayed that Peter's faith would not fail him (see Luke 22:32).

The leaders on the mission field made a mistake and their choices caused pain in my life. It was important for me to forgive them and to continue to honor them. We all make mistakes and we all hurt people from time to time, even when we don't intend to. It is important to show mercy instead of judgment when you are hurt. Our areas of pain can become stumbling blocks or stepping stones in our lives, depending on how we handle these situations.

It is very wise to submit spiritual revelations and interpretations of the Word to an accountability circle of respected leaders to ensure safety. I know of many who have taken the Word, quoted it, and applied it to their lives in deceptive ways. Submission to their leaders for doctrinal accountability would have most likely kept them from error.

Pride is often in the root system of an NFW. Pride is extremely dangerous and can often find a place in a person's life through fear of rejection or failure. It is a defense mechanism that has brought many to ruin. An evil spirit that attaches itself to the sin of pride in believers is the deadly spirit of Leviathan. In Job 41, we find a detailed description of the operations of this evil spirit. Leviathan is referred to in this chapter as the "king of the sons of pride" (v. 34). Verse 15 says that Leviathan's scales are its pride, and verse 26 says that even the sword cannot take him out. In Scripture, the "sword" is symbolic of the Word of God. In our dealings with some NFWs we have found that, when we bring the Word to point out their error, they will often twist its interpretation, or they will talk around the issue. The key to freedom is an absolute commitment to humility. Humility will take out Leviathan. Moving in the opposite spirit from pride is so essential.

An NFW has the potential to cause many problems in a church community if pride is not repented of and replaced by the standard of humility. We have literally seen this "twisted serpent" (Leviathan spirit) attempt to take out entire congregations. It is brutal and very dangerous. Individuals who will not submit to the Word, to authority, or to discipline in a spirit of humility are in danger of walking in terrible deception as well as leading others into it. In cases like this, the individual might need to be released from the prayer group or church.

Philippians 2:1–8 describes the attitude and heart that true spiritual believers should walk in. It describes humility, servanthood, esteeming others and walking in obedience and calls us to have these attitudes in ourselves. Second Timothy 2:24 describes the attitude of God's true servants by saying, *"And the servant of the Lord must not strive; but be gentle unto all men"* (KJV). As we walk in these values, we will grow in favor with God and man. If our ways please the Lord, He will cause even our enemies to be at peace with us (see Prov. 16:7).

You might be wondering at this point, *Oh no! Am I a nut, flake, or weirdo?* Well, why don't you pray and ask the Lord if there is anything in your heart that might need to be adjusted—if so, well then, simply make the adjustment. You are a loved and precious child of God.

Others of you might be thinking, "Oh yeah! *I know* a few of those NFWs." Well, for you I might ask these questions:

- What can *you* do to help them be all that God wants them to be?
- Will you commit yourself to them in prayer or perhaps through counseling, loving confrontation, discipline, and mentoring?
- Are you willing to get to know their heart?

And finally:

- Have you examined your own heart to search it for judgmental, critical, and condescending attitudes? ...Because just maybe *you,* too, are an NFW—and just didn't know it!

It is so important that we do not stand in critical judgment towards anyone, and yet great discernment is needed in these days.

The Kingdom is all about love, **His** love, and do you know what? He loves us all—even if we are a bit nutty, flaky, and even weird at times. He loves us enough to discipline us and lead us into adjustment. Are we willing to walk the processes through with Him? Are we willing to walk the processes through with others?

The passion of the Lord is to see His children living in the fullness of heavenly blessings. Third heaven, angels, and all kinds of other stuff are awaiting us in Him—but more than anything, He wants us to experience the fullness of His love for Him and for each other. Wow, what an invitation to come up higher!

Are you up for it?

Get Ready, Get Set, GO!

So far, the contents of this book have included teaching and testimony regarding heavenly encounters and divine visitations. These are all interesting and intriguing subjects—possibly even entertaining—*but what is it all unto?* Increased devotion and intimacy with Christ is our foremost motivation in encountering realms of glory and visitation, but is there something yet that the Lord would mandate us to before we conclude our study?

A number of years ago our ministry team leaders were discipling a group of zealous young people. They would come together at our home for "Holy Ghost Parties." These were times of soaking in the presence of the Lord and getting "drunk" with Holy Spirit wine. This infilling seemed to ignite them with a fresh passion to reach the lost. Boldness would come upon them to witness. After a time of enjoying the presence, praying, prophesying, and getting filled, they would go out on the streets and begin to share the gospel with the lost. They would come back oftentimes in the early hours of the mornings with great stories of the Lord's power and goodness working through them in their witnessing experiences and "divine appointments."

When you experience realms of the Lord's glory, you will be touched by the things that touch Him. Your heart will break with the very things that break His heart. The fire of His love and glorious presence will transform you and cause you to see people and life differently.

At an intercession meeting for a prophetic conference called "Eyes and Wings," the Lord revealed that He had supernatural encounters planned for the children who were to attend. As we prayed further, we received a strategy for facilitating a move of God amongst them.

During the Saturday morning session of the conference, the young ones were invited to attend a special class tailor-made for them. The Spirit moved in glorious ways. Some were released into visionary experiences and prophetic intercession while others were filled with the Spirit. The Lord was downloading divine empowerment.

That evening in the conference, we invited all the children to the platform. Some were asked to share testimonies. The presence of the Lord fell mightily while they were standing on the stage. Many children fell under the power of the Spirit and various types of manifestations occurred.

One twelve-year-old boy was greatly impacted by the presence of the Lord. He experienced third-heaven encounters as well as visitations from Jesus and His angels. These divine rendezvous produced a profound effect upon this child's life. Within three weeks of the Eyes and Wings conference, this boy had led twelve children in his public school to the Lord. His mother was thrilled with the fruit of the Spirit now evident in her son's life. God had transformed him.

The boy's spiritual visitations had produced a holy boldness in him as well as a fresh hunger to grow in intimate relationship with the Lord. He prayed and praised constantly, reading his Bible and hanging out for hours on end in the War Room (House of Prayer, in Kelowna). This child engaged in passionate intercessory prayer, and was found witnessing to anyone who would listen to him share about Christ. This is just one example of how the Spirit of God continued to visit children—many of them were ignited with flames of love for Christ and led family members and friends to the Lord.

Another example is that of a young man that we are acquainted with, who a few years ago began to engage in some "soaking times" with the Lord. During these hours of worship and basking in the glory presence, he would oftentimes find himself engaging in heavenly visions.

In one particular vision, he saw a specific street corner in his local city where he saw himself witnessing to a man who looked very troubled and dismayed. Through the vision, he was aware of exactly what this person looked like and vividly saw this man being led into a salvation experience. When he came out of the vision, he sensed the Lord had led him to actually go to that specific street corner that very afternoon.

When he arrived on site, he began sharing the message of salvation with those who came by. After an hour or so of handing out gospel tracts, a man approached him who was very discouraged and dejected. To his excitement, it was the very man he had seen in the vision. He proceeded to witness to him in the way he had seen himself doing earlier that day in the heavenly encounter. The man gloriously came to the Lord and was given hope and a new lease on life.

I believe these illustrations vividly demonstrate God's purposes for giving His people experiences in the heavenly realms of glory. It is all about Him! More love, more power, more of Christ and His Kingdom in our lives. The more we are filled, the more we can give. The more we experience, the more we have to share. The more we are empowered by heavenly glory, the more fruit we will produce for Him. We cannot keep His goodness to ourselves. We need to give it out!

I recently had the privilege of meeting a wonderful woman of God. She and her husband are impacting an entire nation in Africa with the love, compassion and tender mercies of the Lord. They are preaching the gospel, healing the sick, working miracles, and caring for the poor every day. Thousands of churches have been planted in the last few years through their ministry, and multitudes are being fed and clothed every month. According to their own testimony, their ministry was bearing very little fruit just a few years ago. What made the difference? Encounters in the glory! Special, divine encounters in God's glory presence over a short period of time dramatically increased their passion and fruitfulness. Impartation from His presence made them ready to ***GO*** into new levels of Kingdom ministry!

This call to fruitfulness is not just for a few. The invitation to experience heavenly glory is not for an elect group. All the fullness of the Kingdom is for **all** believers—it has already been given to us in Christ. Be filled! Be blessed! And then ***GO***! Please ***GO!*** The harvest fields are ripe and white unto harvest. The lost are waiting to be found. They are waiting for ***YOU!***

Following Isaiah's throne room experience, the Lord asked, *"Whom shall I send, and who will go for us?"* Isaiah replied, *"Here am I; send me"* (Isa. 6:8, KJV). Have you experienced the throne room? Like Isaiah, does your heart also respond to God's question with a resounding "send me"?

Get Ready. Soak in His glory, big time, and experience His heavenly blessings on a daily basis. ***Get Set!*** Put things in order and receive your marching orders, and then... ***Go!***

That's what *Third Heaven, Angels... and Other Stuff* is all about. It is about *knowing* Him and it is about *going* with Him to the lost, the hurting, the broken, and the dying. Press on towards that *"upward call of God in Christ Jesus"* (Phil. 3:14). Go for it!

ONWARD AND UPWARD, FRIEND!

Heavenly Father, May Your Kingdom come,
Your will be done, On earth as it is in heaven. Amen.

The Glory School

If you would like to learn more about the glory and experience heavenly encounters, pray about attending the Glory School. The course is taught by Pat Coking and is part of the ministry of Christian Services Association. See our Web site for more information: *www.patcoking.com.*

The following are the lesson titles for the course:

1. The Cross and The Covenant
2. New Creation Realities
3. The Person of The Holy Spirit
4. Faith—The Connector to Heavenly Glory
5. The Word—Our Basis for Experience
6. The Rewards of Holiness
7. Daily Disciplines for Experiencing Heavenly Glory

8. Spiritual Mapping—"Mapping the Throne Zone"
9. Hearing the Voice of God
10. Experiencing the Third Heaven—Part 1
11. Experiencing the Third Heaven—Part 2
12. Angelic Majesties
13. The Fire
14. The Glory
15. Heavenly Provision

About the War Room

Seven Days a Week
HOUSE OF PRAYER
Birthing Global Revival and Harvest

A CALL TO WAR

Revelation 19:11–17 describes Jesus as a Warrior King going forth in authority to wage war in justice and righteousness on behalf of the nations. It also describes His "warrior saints" riding with Him into the battle. A massive global revival and harvest is prophesied in the Scriptures (Hab. 2:14; Isa. 60:1–5; Acts 2:17). This outpouring will be birthed through non-stop and continuous prayer.

Acts 15:16,17 describes the rebuilding of the tabernacle of David (24-hour worship and intercession) *"so that the rest of mankind may seek the Lord, and all the Gentiles who are called by My name"* (v. 17). Revelation chapters 4 and 5 also describes a continual, non-stop flow of worship and intercession before the Lord. In Mark 11:17, Jesus says, *"My house* [place of fixed residence/permanent abode] *shall be called a house of prayer* [intercession] *for all the nations* [heathen/lost]" The Lord is calling many believers worldwide to establish 24-hour intercession movements and houses of prayer.

THE WAR ROOM

The War Room is a prayer room, established through CSA in New Life Church in Kelowna, B.C., Canada in 2001. The room is open with scheduled meetings every day of the week to facilitate intercession for global harvest and revival. Full-time and part-time prayer missionaries labor in the War Room, as well as many dedicated believers who "drop in" to pray when convenient.

WOULD YOU LIKE TO BE INVOLVED?

For more information on our prayer room schedules and how to get involved, check out our web site at *www.patcoking.com.* We are open to training full-time and part-time prayer missionaries. You can also join our e-mail prayer team today!

ABOUT KELOWNA

Kelowna is nestled in the heart of the Okanagan Valley in British Columbia, Canada, which is rich with orchards and vineyards. It is internationally renowned as a resort and tourist destination with plenty of recreational activities available. Swimming, boating, skiing, parasailing, shopping, and golfing are some of the things that tourists enjoy. The majestic Canadian Rockies are only hours away.

On-line Resource Materials

For more available resources, visit us on-line at www.patcoking.com

Various teaching series on audio cassette or CD, and our prayer and teaching manuals, are awaiting you.

Some featured audio-tape items:

F.I.R.E (FERVENT INTERCESSION FOR REVIVAL AND EVANGELISM)

This 22 session series of intercessory prayer teaching is a valuable tool for those desiring to have strong foundational teaching on the subject. Some of the lessons include instruction on: faith, praying the Word of God, prophetic intercession, warfare prayer, the authority of the believer, praying for revival and harvest, travailing prayer, and all manner of prayer.

Prophetic Bootcamp

Stacey Campbell and Pat Coking teach a basic and foundational 10 week study on how to move into the prophetic.

Women in Ministry

This series is a biblical study on women's role in ministry and in the Kingdom of God. This set of 6 tapes includes Pat Coking's personal testimony.

The Glory School

This is an in-depth, 15 lesson study on how to enjoy experience in the glory and third heaven realm. The tape series, with its accompanying manual, is a complementary resource to this book.

The King's Treasury

This cassette series includes powerful teaching on how to receive Kingdom provision in your life. Pat Coking teaches on how to overcome a spirit of lack and poverty.

The Covenant of Love

This single cassette contains one of the most important messages every believer should embrace—the cross of love. If you do not have complete assurance of Christ's unconditional and unfailing love for you, then this teaching is a must.

The Gift Of Tongues

This tape contains over 1 hour of teaching on the gift of tongues and how to receive it. Pat Coking loves to pray for those who feel receiving is difficult. Many have received the gift simply by listening to this tape.